TABLE OF CONTENTS

Truly, when the need is greatest,
then God's help is also always nearest!
Should we not willingly offer our hands
to help where help is still possible?

Blessed Mary Theresa Gerhardinger
Foundress of the Congregation of the School
Sisters of Notre Dame

Foreword

From May, 1944 until April, 1945, Sister Imma Mack made weekly trips to the concentration camp at Dachau in Germany. For almost forty years she kept the memory of these experiences and all that she witnessed a private matter. She herself indicates that it has taken all this time to learn to deal with these »painful memories«. When she finally told some young students what she saw and heard at Dachau, she became eware that what she knew of this tragic time in the history of her country had a message today for other people especially the young.

It is essential in our time that we remember the many ways evil can penetrate and control people, institutions, governments. This was the situation with Hitler's Third Reich. It is as essential to learn how individuals stood against such evil and by the courage of their daily actions brought light into this darkness and, I believe, helped to vanquish it.

WHY I LOVE AZALEAS is another act of love and courage on the part of Sister Imma. While she prefers that her story, her memories be private she has made public this part of her life and how it has affected and transformed her. She has chosen to do this so that others may learn that good can come from evil and that in God all things are possible. As you read this brief account you will also come to know that Sister Imma's sensitivity to the pain and suffering of others enabled her to act in spite of the danger. Her profound faith in God and the support of her family and community sustained her during this time.

I am personally grateful to Sister Imma for this book of her remembrances. Her acts of courage are a message for us to hear God's call in the voices of the oppressed and victimized and to become involved in the work of justice and liberation. This was Jesus' mission and it is our mission. Sister Imma Mack is one person, one women who like Jesus shows the way to go. May her life speak this gospel message to all who read WHY I LOVE AZALEAS.

Sister Patricia Flynn

Sister Patricia Flynn
General Superior of the Congregation
of the Scholl Sisters of Notre Dame

Rome, Italy, July 1991

Preface

We know much about the cruel atrocities carried out in the concentration camp in Dachau during the Nazi era. Only a few of us, however, know how many persons risked their lives to help the prisoners either directly or indirectly.

After receiving many requests to do so, Sister Mary Imma Mack has written her experiences as a young woman going into the concentration camp through the back door which led into the plantation.

It was almost by chance that the then twenty-year-old Josefa came in contact with the concentration camp and the dreadful fate of the prisoners when she was asked to pick up some plants there in May, 1944.

She soon understood what was happening behind the walls and the danger she was putting herself into by going there. Nevertheless, she made the journey from Freising to Dachau week after week, bringing the prisoners bread, comfort and contact with the outside world. Life in the community of the School Sisters of Notre Dame in Freising and her faith in God's direction and protection strengthened her in this venture of love.

11

I am grateful to Sister M. Imma Mack for her willingness to share her personal experiences. Sister M. Alicia Blattenberger deserves special thanks for her help in writing the many impressions and descriptions and for preparing the manuscript.

May this record of lived faith help us to learn from one of the darkest eras of our history and to stay alert and watchful — and may this book give many people, especially young people, courage to move along unknown paths, to feed the hungry, to visit the imprisoned and to bring hope to the despairing.

M. Brigitta Wex

Signed: M. Brigitta Wex
Provincial Superior
Bavarian Province
School Sisters of Notre Dame

October 24, 1988 — Munich, Germany

Author's Preface

Monika Glockann, student advisor at the Technical University in Munich, asked me in July, 1986, to speak about my experiences at the Dachau Concentration Camp to a group of Catholic students and their English guests from the Catholic community of the University of London and to answer their questions. I had been suggested by Father Höck and did not think I ought to decline. She told me that she had already accompanied the group on a visit to the concentration camp at Dachau. The young people had shown great interest in the Carmelite Convent there, much more than in the camp or the explanations in the museum. At first it was obvious that the 30–40 students to whom I was to speak were curious about what a nun would have to say and I could feel their scepticism and reserve. But as the talk continued, they became increasingly interested in my account, and in the end asked many questions.

I was struck by one student's spirited involvement from the very beginning. Thanking me personally afterwards, she said, »During the whole time I was in school, I never wanted to hear anything about National Socialism and especially about the concentration camps. But your eyewitness account has made a deep impression on me.«

I have frequently been asked to record my Dachau experiences and to publish them, especially since 1984, but I have always refused. After meeting these students, however, I began to deal more intensely with my often painful memories and decided to write them down, realizing that it could be helpful especially for young people to hear something firsthand about this chapter in the sinister history of the Third Reich. By then I had also gained sufficient time and space to deal with my memories of those days. May I be forgiven for not going into great detail because I want to give only a very simple account of my experiences.

Preparation for the Assignment

Home and School in Möckenlohe

When I reflect on my trips to the plantation in the Dachau Concentration Camp today, I realize that the events and experiences of my childhood and youth were already a preparation. Telling about these events first will provide background for a better understanding of my story.

I was born in Möckenlohe on February 10, 1924, and baptized Josefa in our parish church. This little village near Eichstätt had approximately 400 inhabitants, mostly farmers. My father, a carpenter, was one of the few skilled workers of the town.

I had just turned nine when Hitler came into power. In my hometown, it was hardly noticed at first. But I do remember that from then on I would often meet Storm Troopers on the road between Eichstätt and Neuburg on the Danube singing the national anthems of the Third Reich, (»Die Fahne hoch ...« and »Deutschland, Deutschland über alles ...«).

15

My own political views were formed at home. Barely ten years old, I was already taking great interest when my father would study the evening newspaper and then talk it over with my mother. Even when I was playing or reading or doing needlework, I would be very alert, listening to these parental conversations, especially when they were about political happenings. I often heard them comment that »hard times are facing us.«

Sometimes my parents would also talk about one or other official who was given an early retirement. It made a deep impression on me when my father would end the conversation with the comment, »He probably wasn't ready to join the party either.« Thus I realized very early that there could be terrible consequences if someone did not join »the Party«. Of course, I really couldn't understand what was happening. I was permitted to receive my First Holy Communion on Low Sunday in 1933. We third graders made our own preparations outside of school time and every now and then would visit a little country chapel on the edge of the village to say our prayers there.

◁ *The Mack Family, with Josefa to the left, Barbara standing, and Josef to the right*

Josefa on her First Communion Day in 1933

On the Saturday before our big day, my friend Marerl and I went into the church to get some holy water. We remained standing in the middle aisle and said our usual prayers aloud. Then Marerl ran off, but for some unknown reason, I stayed standing there a little while. Suddenly I felt God penetrating my very being and addressing me very personally. This experience gave me a feeling of deep happiness. I think that ever since this moment I knew I should give my life to God, but how I was to do that only became clear later.

After Easter vacation I moved up to the fourth grade, which was taught together with the fifth, sixth and seventh grades by Franz Xavier Ruff, the head teacher. Even in school I had a particular interest in anything having to do with Hitler and »the Party«. I remember the teacher repeatedly urging the boys to join the Hitler Youth, but with no success. Actually, he wasn't very insistent either.

I still remember very clearly how one day — I must have been in the fifth or sixth grade — the school superintendent came to our school with a German Girls' Club leader from Eichstätt. We had to go out into the school yard where the woman who accompanied our school superintendent practiced a little dance with us girls. The superintendent, together with the teacher and the boys, watched us and then he said, »If you would join the Hitler Youth or the German Girls' Club, you would have Saturday off, too. The boys could play field games and the girls could learn many more dances«. I remember most of all, however, how the school superintendent kept telling the teacher that he should finally bring himself to get us to join the party's youth organizations. The teacher replied that the superintendent himself should talk with a certain farmer about this. If he would succeed in getting this man to allow his four school age children to join the Hitler Youth, the other parents would probably do the same. The school superintendent, however, refused to follow this advice. I was surprised that the teacher had the courage to talk with the superintendent like that, since I knew from my father's comments how dangerous even the least contradiction could be if it concerned party affairs.

All the school children knew that our pastor, Father Georg Stich, was a »Nazi opponent«. I remember how one day, shortly before religion class, the teacher distributed forms for the parents to sign — forms giving written permission for their children to be accepted into the

Hitler Youth. When the pastor read one such paper, he became indignant. But he really didn't have to get angry since no one in the village gave the requested permission. My mother was so outraged by the paper that she didn't even show it to my father before immediately destroying it.

I got my first new coat in the fall of 1933. A friend of my mother accompanied us to the Guttentag Department Store on Cathedral Square in Eichstätt in order to find the right coat for me. They were both for a green coat, but I wanted a blue one. Mrs. Guttentag, who was Jewish, waited on us herself. She took my side and helped me find the blue coat that I had been longing for. Then she talked with my mother for a long time, and that is how I remember this friendly, helpful woman. It was the only personal contact I had ever had with a Jewish person, but the memory of Mrs. Guttentag only intensified my horror when I heard of the cruel suffering which fell upon the Jewish people during the Hitler era.

It was for this reason, too, that I was deeply shocked by an experience at the end of February, 1934. The upper elementary classes and their teacher had driven to Eichstätt to see a Passion Play being performed by a tour group in the Kolpinghaus (Catholic Youth Center). During the noon hour, because we were familiar with the city, we were allowed to go downtown by ourselves.

I remember how a strange, tense atmosphere prevailed in the streets and alleys. This made me very depressed. Then I heard loud singing. I could only make out a few fragments of the song, but they bored their way into my very being — unforgettably deep: »... your women will wail frightfully and your young girls even more when Jewish blood spurts from the knife ...« I was horrified, and had the impression that this terrible song was being sung all over Eichstätt. The text and melody burned more deeply within me than the scenes from the Passion Play which I had seen earlier. I couldn't understand the gruesome text, but it went through my mind again and again although I wasn't able to talk about it with anyone, even though the depressing memory stayed with me for years.

A strange coincidence occurred many years later. One day in November, 1978, I turned on my radio, wanting to hear a memorial program being broadcast by Bavarian Radio about the »Crystal Night«, November 9–10, 1938, when the synagogues were destroyed. I had hoped to learn something from this program about what had happened, having heard absolutely nothing at the time it occurred. The program had barely begun when I was startled by rough voices singing that terrible song which had so deeply wounded my whole being as a child in Eichstätt in 1934. I had not heard it since then, and now it began to resound in my ears again, a cruel and violent reawakening of this dreadful childhood experience.

Our teacher finally managed to get a small group of volunteers to join the Hitler Youth during the summer of 1936, but there wasn't a single girl among them. One sunny Saturday morning the rest of us were sitting in our classroom, quiet as mice. We saw and heard how these boys were singing as they marched toward the forest. The teacher came into the classroom, sat down as usual on the first bench and nervously tapped his trouser leg with his cane. After a few minutes of oppressive silence he said, »The Hitler Youth can march into the forest and play there all morning. You have to sit in school and paint and read.« In no way did that make me unhappy. I thought to myself instead, »I'd much rather do this.« As a country girl I had sufficient opportunity to romp about outdoors after school hours.

By the end of 1936, however, we — like the young people in all of Germany — were automatically enrolled in the Hitler Youth and the German Girls' Club. But that did not mean any »political change« for us school girls from Möckenlohe because Josefa Hirsch was our leader. This teacher was born in our village and had genuinely held on to the basic convictions of her village community. She would play, sing and hike with us, or read and do crafts and needlework, depending on the season. »Political instruction,« the real task, was completely ignored by our leader, so I wasn't under any pressure as a result of my »German Girls' Club duty«.

Candidate with the School Sisters of Notre Dame

I had an aunt who worked as a needlework teacher in the convent of the School Sisters of Notre Dame in Pfaffenhofen on the Ilm River. After I had completed elementary school, I went there in December, 1937, to learn how to cook and to do the shopping. There, as in all the other convents of the School Sisters, I found the same political views as those I had been accustomed to in my parents' home — explicit, absolute rejection. The Nazi regime was hostile to the convents from the very beginning. Early in 1937, religious teachers were banished from almost all the elementary schools, and the teachers' training schools belonging to religious communities were closed, one after another. The Sisters were also expelled from most of the kindergartens, homes for children, and day homes for school children, as well as from all secondary schools.

I had hardly arrived in Pfaffenhofen when I received a letter postmarked Eichstätt which had been forwarded to me. It contained the notification that I was named the German Girls' Club leader in Möckenlohe. I became very frightened and gave the letter to the Sisters to read. After giving it some thought, they said, »The best thing would be to completely ignore it.« That was good advice since I never received another letter in this regard. My repeated change of schools and address probably kept me from being registered with the German Girls' Club.

Because I expressed my desire to become a School Sister like my aunt some day, the Sisters sent me to the convent boarding school at Gaimersheim near Ingolstadt in September, 1938. Here I was to be prepared for the needlework teachers' training school. The curriculum in this school was equivalent to that given in the middle schools after the war. Emphasis was placed on commercial subjects, but much time was also given to needlework and home economics.

Since I had decided to become a candidate with the School Sisters of Notre Dame, my father brought me to the Anger Convent in Munich in April, 1940. I was to receive my training at our school for needlework teachers in Munich-Au, but already in January, 1942, the Sisters in leadership had to tell us that by reason of a national decree, students in convent schools were not permitted to take the national examinations. Either we had to say that we would leave the convent and attend the municipal training school in the future, or make the decision to stay in the candidature and learn nursing. The convent on Mariahilf Square had already been confiscated by the armed forces for use as an auxiliary military hospital in October, 1941, and more rooms were taken over in January, 1942. Since there wasn't any more room for us candidates in the convent in Munich-Au, we all went to the Motherhouse in Munich.

Sister M. Mechtild Wüst, directress of Candidates at the time, didn't think I had what it takes to be a nurse. After consulting me, she made the suggestion to Mother M. Almeda, our General Superior, that I be sent to Saint Clara's, a mission in Freising, where I could minister as an assistant in the children's home, and, as much as duties would allow, learn dressmaking from Sister M. Warina Brenninger. The Sisters thought that this training would certainly be of great benefit in my later profession as a needlework teacher, since there was always the hope that one day the Sisters would be able to return to the schools. Mother M. Almeda agreed; and so in April, 1942, I arrived in Freising, where I began working full-time with the school girls in the children's home and

practicing tailoring on the side. Sister M. Saba Gigl, the local leader, was even able to obtain recognition of my previous training in the needlework teachers' school from the Apprentice Commission of the Dressmakers' Trade Guild. Thus I was permitted to take my final apprentice's examination already in January, 1943.

I was supposed to be summoned to the National Labor Service in the summer of 1943. Mayor Hans Lechner, who was very favorably disposed to the School Sisters, obtained my deferment from the responsible party functionaries by declaring very energetically that I was indispensable in the care of the orphans.

During these troubled times, my desire to become a School Sister of Notre Dame became even stronger, so in December, 1943, I asked Mother M. Almeda Schricker, General Superior at the time, for permission to enter the novitiate during the following summer. I was accepted for reception in August, 1944, and it seemed as if the longing of my childhood and youth would soon be fulfilled. But something else was to come instead. Because of the war,

◁ *Josefa with the children in the home at Freising*

reception could not be held in 1944; and the doors of the novitiate were first opened for me in the summer of 1945. In the meantime I was confronted with a very difficult and dangerous task which I could never have imagined, even in a dream — that of bringing a little comfort and help to the many prisoners in the concentration camp in Dachau, a place about which I had known hardly anything until then.[1]

---

[1] See Appendix

Experiences During My Trips
to the Plantation

The Task

One evening in the middle of May, 1944,
I was spending some free time with the other
candidates in the garden at Saint Clara's when
Sister Saba had me called to her office. There
she introduced me to Mr. Dür, a well digger from
Freising, a man well-known to the Sisters. I
learned that he had worked together with a
group of prisoners from the concentration
camp in Dachau for years. He told us that these
men suffered great hunger in the camp. Sister
Saba promised to help as much as possible.
She also told me that Mr. Dür had been getting
bread for the prisoners from our convent for a
long time. After sharing this, she asked me to
go with one of the schoolgirls into the concentration camp at Dachau the next day. We were
to pick up the vegetables and flower plants
which Mr. Dür had ordered for Saint Clara's
from the camp's market garden. Smiling, she
added, »You don't need to be afraid; you won't

see much of the concentration camp.« At the moment, I could understand only a little of what that all meant.

After Mr. Dür had given me a few tips for the journey, I could go back to the garden again. On the way I met Sister M. Adula Niebauer and told her that I was to go to the concentration camp at Dachau the next day. She was shocked by what I said and whispered with great consternation, »Speak softly! There are political prisoners there. My cousin, Father Ludwig Spießl, is also a prisoner in Dachau. If you see him, greet him for me.«

In spite of the good Sister's anxious warning, I never gave a thought as to what kind of clothing I should wear when I went to the concentration camp. I just wore what we had during that time of need - a colored dress in summer, and a strawberry red and beige checkered jacket when it rained. Of course I needed a better outfit during the winter, something hard to find at the time.

Plantation with the camp buildings ▷

Prisoners in Dachau

First Encounters and Impressions

On Tuesday, May 16, 1944, my companion and I took the train to Dachau by way of Munich. We arrived a little before eleven and headed for the camp at once. After a good half hour, we met Mr. Dür, waiting for us in the SS-barracks with a large handcart, just as we had arranged previously. We were to take the hand-cart with the plants which had been ordered to the train station. He would pick up the vehicle later.

Mr. Dür accompanied us to the camp market garden, the so-called »plantation,« this first time. We went down the wide »SS-Road« until we reached Eicke Square. To the left, behind cultivated gardens, we saw villas beautifully decorated with flowers in window boxes. Mr. Dür told us that the SS-leaders and their families lived there. The flowers would have come from the market garden.

After we had crossed the square at the end of the long road, we continued along a bumpy path. We passed two barracks with a huge pile of old shoes lying in front. The odor was dreadful. We could see men with shaved heads working on the shoes behind the windows. I was already shocked.

To the right of these barracks lay the large fields where small groups of prisoners were working. A guard was standing by each group.

The men had just finished their work and were lining up on the commando road for roll call, Mr. Dür quietly explained to us. I found the sight distressing — hundreds of men in zebra-striped trousers and jackets or in shabby civilian clothes, their heads shaved, their pale faces bloated and puffy. Everybody stared at us as if we were creatures from another world. I will never be able to forget this sight.

After we had passed the prisoners, we finally came to the shop, a small office where Father Schönwälder, a young prisoner from the Sudetenland, sold flowers, plants and seeds to the customers. The room was annexed to a greenhouse where Father Schönwälder was already waiting for us. In a rather unfriendly tone he said that we would have to be a little patient and wait until the plants were ready. I was still so shocked by the sight of the prisoners that his somewhat brusque manner

Entrance to the plantation with the shop ▷

made absolutely no impression on me. I told him that we would be glad to wait since we couldn't go home until later anyway. He took us into the shop where he said we could sit down until the plants were packed. Meanwhile he would write out the bill.

While I was waiting, I ventured to ask whether he knew a Father Ludwig Spießl, the brother of a School Sister. He brushed me aside, quickly whispering that I should speak more quietly, that the guard at the door was watching him very carefully, and that he was only permitted to talk about business matters with civilians. Of course he knew Ludwig Spießl. He would be happy to give him the greetings which I brought from Sister Adula.

Gradually the prisoner's overly cautious manner toward me disappeared, and he excused himself for his unfriendliness. He explained that he had wanted to gain time to observe me. However, since I talked with him very openly, his mistrust quickly vanished. Then he told me about life in the camp, about hunger and punishments, about deprivation and death, and

◁ *Prisoners on the camp road*

especially about the hatred for priests and religion. I could not believe that such a thing was possible in Germany. It was unfathomable. Only later on did I begin to comprehend conditions little by little because many other prisoners told me about the same or similar harassment and ill-treatment. When we said good-by, Father Schönwälder took me aside, asked me to come again, and, if possible, bring along some hosts and a bottle of wine so that his companion priests from Poland could celebrate Eucharist in secret. I had to firmly promise that I would tell no one except my local leaders about what I had seen and experienced in Dachau. He had not yet finished speaking when the door suddenly opened and an SS-man walked in. I was terrified, but Father Schönwälder said in a quiet, businesslike manner, »Good-by. You can pick up the plants which you ordered on Tuesday.«

Deeply shaken, depressed and sad, I went home with my companion, who apparently had understood very little of what was happening. I could hardly wait to tell Sister Saba and Sister Vigoris, our candidates' directress, about the horrible experience and the dreadful things I had seen and heard. The Sisters, too, were shocked and grief-stricken, and immediately began to think about ways in which we could help even more.

I went through the next days as if walking in my sleep. As a child I had voraciously read stories about the martyrs during the first centuries of Christianity and had been especially impressed by the help the selfless Christians gave one another. At the time a quiet longing rose within me, a desire to help people who were in distress because of their faith, just as the early Christians did. This longing never left me, just the opposite, it grew stronger with the years. The thought would not leave me: »What's happening now in Dachau is just like the times of the early church. This is a real persecution of Christians.« I became more and more certain that the time had come for my childhood longing to be fulfilled, that I was being challenged by the present circumstances to act with total selflessness.

A week later, I went to Dachau alone, something which I was to do many times until the American troops freed the prisoners at the end of April, 1945. I made these dangerous journeys with a great inner assurance, but even more so, with the confident trust that my life was secure in God's loving care. My local leaders gave me permission to make this second journey as well as all succeeding ones which were prompted by the situations emerging from week to week. Father Schönwälder was very much pleased when I came again. It was proof for him that he could trust me. He had even prepared the flowers and plants ahead of time for me to take along. The minute I could see through the window that the guard was some distance away, I gave him the Mass wine, the hosts and the mail for Father Spießl from Sister Adula.

On this particular day, Father Schönwälder was still waiting for some SS-men who had ordered bouquets and wanted to pick them up soon. Therefore he couldn't let me wait in the little shop and sent me into the adjoining greenhouse. There I met a prisoner who was about 60 years old and we started talking immediately. He told me that he was a religious from the diocese of Münster and that conditions were still relatively good for the German prisoners since they were permitted to get packages from their families. They would share them with the others, too, but those who weren't German, especially prisoners from Poland and Russia, were suffering very much from hunger. If it were possible, I was to bring along food, especially bread. We had not been speaking very long when a whole group of prisoners gathered around us. At first they stared at me as if I were an apparition, but then they wanted to know where I had come from. I very willingly told them that I was a candidate with the School Sisters in Freising. The prisoners, who were just then having their short noon break, could not tell me enough about life in the camp. They were all excited, and everyone was talking at once. I don't remember much of what they said — I must have tried to suppress it. Otherwise I would have probably had the burden of knowing about such cruelty and horror for the rest of my life. There were accounts of unbelievable humiliation, harassment, torture and cruelty similar to that described by Adalbert Ludwig Balling in his book, »LEAVING BEHIND A TRACE OF LOVE« (Eine Spur der Liebe hinterlassen, Mariannhill Missionary Press, Würzburg, 1984). It seemed as if the men had a great need to tell about their deprivation and torture in detail to someone coming from the outside. The final comment was, »If we would ever really be set free again, no one would believe what we have experienced here.«

When Father Schönwälder brought me back into the shop, he asked me to come again and enumerated various things that I was to bring along. His requests were always oral and I never got a written list from him. But later on he did give me notes from his own experiences. Before I said good-by, he also asked me to take some letters from the prisoners and mail them in Freising. He had to make it clear to me, however, that there was a death penalty for carrying illegal letters to and from the camp, but I promised to carry out his request anyway.

On the way home I was overcome by a deep depression. The prisoners' stories of the inhumanities in Dachau finally made me completely aware of what was happening there. For the first time, I realized that these men had been sentenced to imprisonment in the Dachau Concentration Camp almost exclusively for political reasons. Coming home, I reported on my latest experiences. Sister Saba and Sister Vigoris were deeply moved, especially by the fact that the prisoners from Poland and Russia had to suffer such terrible hunger. They saw to it that whenever possible on my next trips, I would be able to take food for these poorest of the poor.

At this time, we four candidates at Saint Clara's were practicing a little play for a coming feast day. However, because of my deep depression, I did not feel I could take part. Sister Vigoris understood, and the play was canceled.

»Mädi« — An Assumed Name
New Experiences

During the following weeks, I went to Dachau again according to prearranged plans, bringing along black bread and white bread and even some ham and butter. It was too dangerous for me to give these to Father Schönwälder, so he sent me into the adjoining greenhouse again, where I gave the food directly to the prisoners from Poland. They were overjoyed and never grew weary of thanking me.

On this particular day I met Father Stanislaus, a Capuchin from Poland who was about 30 years old. From this time on he played a very important role in accepting and delivering the food which I brought. I asked him why there were so many Polish priests in the concentration camp in Dachau. He told me that it was because the Nazis wanted to exterminate the Polish intellectuals. Hearing that, I was again shocked and distressed. Father Stanislaus also explained the meaning of the squares of cloth in various colors which were sewn onto the prisoners' jackets.

As I was about to leave, Father Schönwälder again asked me to return, adding that from then on he would just call me »Mädi«. It would be too dangerous to use my own name. For a moment I rebelled against this assumed name, but I soon got used to it. Maybe Father Schönwälder came up with the name »Mädi« because I still looked so young, almost like a little girl. I wore my hair in braids arranged around my head as most of the candidates did at the time. Even when my prefect advised me to have my hair cut so I wouldn't be so conspicuous, I wouldn't do it, since I didn't want to change the hair style that seemed to be just right for me.

The prisoners were indescribably happy that I would come again and again. Whenever they had a chance just to see me, they would cordially greet me.

An incident occurred during my third trip to Dachau at the end of May. As, lost in thought, I was going toward Saint Clara's from the train station, a soldier approached me. He explained he was a classmate who had been stationed in the barracks there for a few weeks. Curious, he asked me where I had been. »In Dachau,« I replied, but gave him no further explanation. Soon after that, Michael went home for vacation and told my parents that he had met me and that I had just come from Dachau.

Now I was going to Dachau every week. At first I took the train by way of Munich and then walked from the train station to the plantation. One day the train stopped in Moosach and the conductor announced, »Everybody out! The train can't go on to Munich because the main train station has been bombed.« I stood on the platform, not knowing what to do. In one hand I had a heavy sack, in the other a market basket filled with food for the prisoners. Then I had an idea that saved the day. »Now if you go down this street, you will get to Allach where you can probably take the next train to Dachau.« No sooner said than done! The streets were totally deserted and I was carrying a heavy load.

On the way to the station, a woman met me. What a mutual surprise! She was my father's cousin! She assured me that I was going the right way, but she was very astonished to find me there and all alone. When she asked where

I was going, I answered truthfully, »To Dachau.« I didn't give her any more details; and fortunately, she didn't ask any more questions either. When this cousin was on vacation in Möckenlohe in late autumn, 1944, she told my parents about having met me in such strange circumstances and that I had said that I was going to Dachau.

Weeks later on the train, I met a friend of my parents who was on his way to Möckenlohe to do some »storing up.« He, too, reported at home that he had met me and that I was on my way to Dachau. At Christmas I heard about the repercussions and my parents' understandable consternation over these three pieces of information that seemed very peculiar to them.

The disrupted railway connections made my return trip from Dachau to Freising just as exhausting as the morning journey. I told about my adventure at home. Since the prisoners had again asked for various things and were counting on my coming again the following week, Sister Saba, Sister Vigoris and I thought about what would be the best way to travel to Dachau in the given circumstances. We thought it might be better to take the bicycle on the train as far as Schleißheim and then to ride about ten kilometers on the fairly level road from there to Dachau. The first trip already proved that we had found a good solution. Now I didn't need to walk a great distance, and thus could carry a far greater load. This load did indeed become heavier from week to week. Whatever the Sisters were able to spare by way of food was gathered for the poor prisoners in Dachau, who accepted it with great gratitude.

Packages were loaded into the luggage carrier. I could even hang some more fully packed bags on the two handlebars. The only difficulty I had was in getting on and off the train, since I had to check the bicycle in the baggage car but take the packages and bags into the compartment. I was always lucky, because nothing was ever stolen from the things which I had to set down when I checked my bicycle or picked it up later.

Since it was too dangerous to keep delivering such a large amount of food in the small, carefully guarded shop or even in the adjoining greenhouse, Father Schönwälder soon found another solution. He had known the Beer family from the time he was a student in Warsaw. They now lived across from the plantation in the administration building, where Mr. Beer, a widower and father of five children, worked as a bookkeeper in the market garden offices. Father Schönwälder had made arrangements with his daughter, Toni, for me to deliver all the food to the Beer family from then on. Camouflaged to look like laundry, it would then be picked up by Polish prisoners coming through a storage exit. Father Stanislaus, whom I already knew, assumed responsibility for this undertaking.

I soon came to know and trust Toni Beer, who was only a few years older than I, but I met her father only sometime later. From the very beginning he appeared to be a very serious, uncommunicative man, and I was always somewhat afraid of him. I couldn't help getting the impression that he was only reluctantly tolerating the delivery of food for the prisoners from his apartment.

When the Sisters met Toni during a visit in Freising, they too were impressed with her. A camaraderie developed between the two of us.

Several times during air raids, she took me into the shelter where most of the people seeking refuge were the wives and children of SS-men. It was a severe strain on my nerves each time I was together with them, since the prisoners who had to do housework for

SS-families had told me how they had been cruelly harassed in their apartments many times.

When I came to the camp once again at the end of June, Father Schönwälder, happy and excited, welcomed me by saying, »Mädi, we're coming to Freising next Sunday!« I was surprised and couldn't imagine how that was supposed to happen. But it was true! Father Schönwälder really did come, accompanied by Mr. Gaster, an Austrian officer who had been imprisoned in Dachau for six years, and a commander, about whom Father Schönwälder had told me previously. This Nazi from the Sudetenland was between 50 and 60 years of age and treated the prisoners humanely, even doing them some services.

The three men drove rickety bicycles along the bumpy country roads from Dachau to Freising. Tired and hungry, they arrived at Saint Clara's about 9:30 a.m. Father Schönwälder immediately celebrated Eucharist. Mr. Gaster was the server. The commander was given a substantial breakfast in the meantime, since it was only his goodwill that let him be talked into risking the dangerous journey with the two men. The prisoners' stories gave Sister Saba and Sister Vigoris firsthand insight into the misery of camp life.

That afternoon, our visitors said good-by with great sadness. By then the Sisters had loaded up the bicycles with food. Grateful for the goods received and hoping that they could come again soon, they returned to the camp. They actually dared to make the dangerous journey three more times, with Father Stanislaus from Poland coming in place of Mr. Gaster both the next and the last time. He showed us the deeply scarred perforations in his legs which were the result of the experimentally induced infection which he had survived. Deeply moved, he later told me over and over again how very touched he had been by the love and concern of the Sisters.

The prisoners wore their uniforms when they went on their dangerous and adventuresome journeys. The 20–30 centimeter high letters, KL[2], were scrawled in red paint on the backs of their jackets. The commander wore his Nazi uniform. They had »organized« the bicycles for themselves. The men had agreed that in case they were checked, they would say that they

[2] See Appendix

were a small work detail who had an outside task to fulfill. But, thanks be to God, all went well each time.

In the summer of 1944, when the flowers in the plantation were blooming in all their splendor, Mr. Gaster brought a whole basket of magnificent gladiolus »for Freising« to Father Schönwälder on the days when I was expected. I was never allowed to pay for them. They were a gift from the prisoners who wanted to show their gratitude for the goods they had received. Thus we could decorate the chapel with the most beautiful flowers from the SS-plantation all summer and autumn.

Once during this time, Father Schönwälder also asked whether I could bring along about 700 hosts each week. If I could bring them, the Polish priests could secretly celebrate Eucharist while they were on work assignments in the plantation, using the very simple rite permitted by Rome. Sister Saba readily approved, ordering flour from the farm in Freising to be sent to the School Sisters in Dorfen who had a host bakery.

A Dangerous Situation

At the beginning of July, I was on the way to the plantation once again when the first guard that I had to pass stopped me with no warning whatsoever. I was filled with terror. That had never happened before. I got off the bicycle and stood there. Appearing to be friendly, the young SS-guard told me that he would like to chat with me a little. It was boring to have to stand guard on such a beautiful day. He would much rather go walking with me. In a flash I thought to myself, »Now if you would react in the same friendly manner, you will surely arouse less distrust than if you gave him the cold shoulder.« So I stayed there for a few minutes and talked with him.

Whenever Father Schönwälder was expecting me, he would send a 14–16 year old Polish boy down the road to watch for me. Now on this particular day, Max saw me standing by the guard and immediately reported it in the shop. When I arrived a few minutes later, I met Father Schönwälder who was very upset. I told him that I had talked a little with the guard but that he had not checked me. Father Schönwälder wouldn't calm down and, infuriated, said to me,

»Mädi, if they'd ever catch you, you'd betray all of us!« In a momentary act of defiance, but proudly, too, I thought to myself, »And even if they'd kill me, I wouldn't betray anybody.«

While I could understand Father Schönwälder in a way, it was still very frightening. Until then I had experienced him as an almost cold-blooded man who wasn't afraid of taking any kind of risk. Once he had told me, for example, how he had gone out from the plantation, past the guards and into the camp with two pails filled with »organized« things. As we continued talking, he asked me for forgiveness. Nevertheless, his remark that he had been almost literally frightened to death affected me deeply.

This experience went through my mind once again on the way home. I couldn't help thinking over and over again, »If you'd get caught, they'd find out where you're coming from.« The thought that the Sisters would then be dragged into my case disturbed me profoundly. Until then I had not been fully conscious of the fact that Saint Clara's was also in danger because of me.

But it was impossible for me to talk about it. Sister Vigoris noticed that I was disturbed and wanted to know what was bothering me.

I couldn't tell her and made up various excuses but she wouldn't accept them. As we were packing the things for the prisoners on the evening before my next trip to Dachau, she put pressure on me with the remark, »I'm not going to let you go if you don't tell me what's wrong.« Desperately I thought to myself, »But I can't tell her that I'm afraid for her and the other Sisters. Then for sure she won't let me go ... but the prisoners are waiting for me.« So I remained silent. Tension reigned as we each went our way.

The next morning we loaded up my bicycle in silence. Not another word was said about the threatened refusal to let me go. But this time there weren't any incidents on the journey either. This helped me cope with the experience of the previous week. When I returned home, I was once again able to tell how the day went and the inner tension subsided to »normal«.

One morning Sister Adula said in her kind and motherly way, »Josefa, you're sleeping so restlessly these days. You're talking and

◁ *Concentration camp barracks at Dachau*

thrashing around in your sleep.« I told her that I certainly wouldn't remember that, but that I actually had been having bad dreams lately. Even though we didn't talk about it, she knew why. We slept in little curtained cubicles in the dormitory with the preschool girls, so she was a witness of my nocturnal unrest and worried about me.

God Shows the Way

In July, I had to deal with a very personal problem. My reception was scheduled for August. I didn't want to step back, but I didn't want to stop going to Dachau either. So I wanted both and didn't think I could give up either of them. I became more and more conscious of the fact that my trips to Dachau were like a compelling demand which was interrupting my life. Could I withdraw now without feeling guilty? This question turned into a difficult struggle over my decision of the previous December. What should I do in this inner conflict? To whom should I turn for advice? Father Gustav von Mann-Tiechler came to Saint Clara's from Freiburg during this time of inner confusion. I trusted him and talked over my problem with him. He listened very thoughtfully and then said, »Continue going to Dachau. The rest will take care of itself.« This dialogue brought me inner peace.

Shortly after that, I received a pleading letter from my father. He wrote, »In August you are going to the novitiate in Munich where there is constant bombing? You can't do that to us. Whoever can, flees the city, and you want to go

59

there? You simply may not do that!« I talked with Sister Vigoris about this letter and she answered just like the priest from Freiburg: »This problem will solve itself.« I felt strengthened in my newly restored inner peace.

A day or two later, a letter came from the Generalate. Mother M. Almeda had written, »Because of the heavy bombing attacks on Munich, reception is being postponed until further notice.« The problem had really solved itself.

A Faithful Helper in Risky Negotiations

At the end of June I was given a letter in Dachau for our chaplain, Father Peter Eichten, a Redemptorist who had been evacuated from Bochum and who was living in a house on the convent property at Saint Clara's. I gave it to him personally and he was stunned by this mail from his brother Redemptorists imprisoned in the Dachau Concentration Camp. I briefly explained to him how I got this letter. Father Eichten's joy was so great that I was very moved when I left.

At the door I met Erich Berschtl, a Jesuit brother employed at our house, who was on his way to to see Father Eichten. The next morning he wanted to talk to me and told me that the priest in tears, had told him, that I had brought him an illegal letter from another Redemptorist imprisoned in Dachau. I was extremely terrified, since I had asked Father Eichten to say nothing about the matter. Brother Erich excused the priest with the remark, »But he was so taken up with this happy surprise that he simply had to talk. And that was the only thing that made it possible for me to talk with you about my former novice master.« Then he told me that Father Otto Pies had been in the Dachau Concentration Camp for some years already, but he had never been able to contact him. He wanted to ask me if I would take a letter to Father Pies. I said I would.

The next time I went to Dachau, I already had a letter with me from Brother Erich. But first I cautiously asked Father Schönwälder about the Jesuit. His response was, »Father Pies is known throughout the whole camp. He is a very important figure among the priests.« Then I secretly slipped him the letter and told him who had given it to me. He added that Father Pies worked in the market garden and he would think up a way for him to come to the shop during my next visit so that I could meet him personally and speak with him about Brother Erich.

This news made Brother Erich very happy and he gave me a letter for his imprisoned novice director the next week also. When I was in the shop, a prisoner came in with a flower pot. Father Schönwälder whispered to me that he was Father Pies and that he would like to talk with me a little. I gave him the letter and told him very briefly that Brother Erich was helping out with the harvest at Saint Clara's. Father Pies asked if Brother Erich could perhaps come along on the next trip. I told him that we would have to borrow a bicycle for him and then perhaps it might be possible.

I talked it over with Sister Saba and Sister Vigoris at home first. After a while we called for Brother Erich. In his great concern for Father Pies, he was very happy about what I had to tell him and very enthusiastic about the plan of going with me on my next trip to Dachau.

As we traveled together during the following week, I asked Brother Erich why he, a young man, wasn't in the army, but permitted to study part-time instead and obliged to help us with the harvest. He told me in great detail that according to a decree from Hitler during the summer of 1941, the Jesuits »were not worthy to serve in the German army.« He had been a soldier, but was dismissed one day for that reason.

The meeting with Father Pies in Dachau really did take place to the great happiness of both. The two could talk about important things, and, most of all, Father Pies could provide information about the other Jesuits imprisoned in Dachau.

A few weeks later, Brother Erich went with me to Dachau once again. On the way home, my companion wanted to know what I planned to do someday. I told him that I would like to become a School Sister.

Then he proceeded to explain the vows to me and especially the difference between »simple« and »solemn« vows. I don't think that I understood much about this difference because Dachau was still constantly on my mind. While we were waiting in Schleißheim for the train to Freising, I took a couple pears that my mother had sent me out of my pocket. They were »Good Greys«, a variety with a rough peeling but still very juicy and tasty. I shared the pears with Brother Erich and we enjoyed them together. After the tension in Dachau, it was a delicious treat for both of us. When Brother Erich had eaten his share, he said jokingly, »The next time you go home, give special greetings to the pear tree! It's done its job well.«

All summer long, Brother Erich stored up supplies from the area around Freising. Our kitchen-personnel would make various baked goods from whatever flour, butter, sugar and eggs he could get, since they were easier to pack and would keep better in the camp. Thus he was able to send a large number of packages to his Jesuit brothers imprisoned in Dachau before he went back to Maria Eck in September for his theology studies.

It was the middle of summer. I was in Dachau again and was just whispering something to Father Schönwälder when the door to the shop opened. A young SS-man came in and said that he had been told to pick up the bridal bouquet which had been ordered. A prisoner brought the very beautifully arranged bouquet. The SS-man took it, turned to me and very spontaneously placed it in my arms. Then he said a few niceties like, »You're so pretty. You'd make a charming bride.« For a moment I was too surprised and frightened to speak. But then the sight of his friendly and sincere face quickly dissolved the tension. Smiling, I gave the bouquet back to him without a word.

I had already carried letters for Father Spießl from time to time. He told me through Father Schönwälder that I should arrange for him to meet his sister. I was able to do this, much to the joy of all of us. On August 18th, I took part in a Profession Ceremony in Weichs where Sister M. Klodulfa Spießl was missioned. The next day she accompanied me to Dachau, wearing lay clothing. The brother and sister were able to speak together briefly in Father Schönwälder's shop. Now, more than forty years later, Father Spießl remembers this meeting to the tiniest detail. An excerpt from his account written to me on January 15, 1987, reads:

»... One day Ferdinand Schönwälder came to me with special greetings from Sister Adula, a cousin of mine in Freising. They had been brought by "Mädi", a candidate with the School Sisters there, who sometimes came to "shop" for vegetables. They had already been

Father Ludwig Spießl

thinking that my sister, Sister Klodulfa from Weichs, could come along on one of these "shopping trips" — in lay clothing, of course — and that a meeting with me could be made possible. Saturday, the 19th of August, was thought to be a good day since the SS-men weren't so assiduous about checking anymore on Saturdays.

By Easter, 1944, I had been promoted to senior rank in the barracks in Block 26/3, since it seemed that I had been in the camp the longest and that I knew a number of "helpful bits of information." Now I had to take the place of one of my companions in the plantation commando, since the number had to be correct. When I was absent, I had a substitute in the barracks — as is common in military operations. I said to him, "In case a guard comes to check and asks about me, you can tell him that I am gone for a sun-ray treatment. I had survived double pleurisy in spring, so, of course, a natural "sun-ray treatment" couldn't hurt me. Fortunately my substitute did not need to use this embellishment of the truth — not exactly sinful, but not exactly innocent either — because no guard ever came.

So I went to the plantation and met Schön-wälder's group in the greenhouse. Here I was given some kind of busy work as a cover-up in case there was a »visit.« When the two women came in »to shop,« the coast was clear. Our greeting at such a reunion was intentionally very matter-of-fact and the conversation brief to avoid causing a stir among the prisoners working across from us. Convincing my sister that I had recovered sufficiently to hold out a little longer until the war would finally end, which indeed it had to, was crucial to the meeting.

For my parents, brothers and sisters, this kind of personal information would certainly carry much more weight than the stereotype sentence, "Am in good health, and so far everything is going well," which had to appear in the twice-monthly letters in order for them to get through the censor.

May I therefore personally and sincerely thank you once again today for the worthy Good Samaritan service which you performed for all of us by taking on such a risky venture. We knew very well how dangerous that must have been for you personally, for our cousin, Sister Adula, too, and perhaps even for your house. Besides that, there were also the valuable food supplies which you brought on each of your errands, on your bicycle trips from Freising ..."

Signed: Ludwig Spießl, Pastor

After this successful meeting with her brother, Sister Klodulfa returned to Weichs, and I took the usual way back to Freising.

Father Schönwälder received more and more illegal letters from the prisoners for me to deliver. I stamped them at home and put them into various mailboxes. One day he had to tell me, however, that the strict orders regarding mail would be carried out again with much greater severity than in the past. Once again attention was drawn to the fact that it was absolutely and strictly forbidden to smuggle illegal letters out of the camp. Whoever still did so should be ready for the death sentence. With this in mind, Father Schönwälder thought that I shouldn't come for two weeks, but we did set a definite date for my next trip.

Three or four days later, Sister Saba had Sister Vigoris call me to her office. On the way she told me there was a woman there who wanted to speak to "Mädi". The woman, who was in her mid-forties, introduced herself as Mrs. Steinbüchler from Amperweg No. 38, Dachau. She said that she was to give greetings from a Mr. Schönwälder, if that meant anything to me. »Of course I know him,« I answered. »He is the prisoner in the plantation shop in the concentration camp in Dachau.« Mrs. Steinbüchler told us that her ten-year-old daughter Christl had been at the market garden. Father Schönwälder had given her a little slip of paper for me as well as my address here in Freising. There was a short note on the paper saying that instead of coming only after two weeks as previously arranged, I should come next week and bring a certain kind of medication for typhoid fever.

Sister Saba was actually able to obtain the medicine, making it possible for me to fulfill the request. The next time I saw Father Schönwälder, he told me that typhoid fever had broken out in the camp. Many prisoners were sick, and some had already died. For this reason, the prisoners had decided to put aside all caution regarding letters. He asked me to bring as much medicine as possible. When I reported that to Sister Saba, she sent a few Sisters into the various drugstores in Freising in order to get the medicine. They didn't want me to have anything to do with obtaining the medication. Each time I went to Dachau from then on, I would bring not only food but also the various medications until the camp was taken over by the Americans.

One day I was given a letter in the camp for Father Kaspar Quirmbach, a Pallottine Father who was chaplain in the Vincentian Home for the Elderly near the Munich Chapel in Freising. I had known him already from conferences which he had given for teachers in our chapel. Because he was not available, I could not personally give him the letter from his Pallottine brother imprisoned in Dachau. Later, however, he himself came to Saint Clara's to find out more details about how the letter got to him. At the same time he also said that he would like to go with me to Dachau once so that he might possibly meet his companion brother.

On my next trip, Father Schönwälder informed me that this particular Pallottine Father worked in the »pepper mill«[3] and could not come to the shop, but that perhaps we could go into this building quite inconspicuously and find him there. Shortly after that, Father Quirmbach accompanied me to Dachau once and we were able to go into the pepper mill without being noticed. The joy at seeing one another again was great, and both priests were able to

[3] See Appendix

talk to one another briefly. Afterwards Father Quirmbach also wanted to visit a family he knew in Dachau. I used the opportunity to accept Mrs. Steinbüchler's invitation. Thus I met her two daughters, Anneliese and Christl, who was the younger of the two. Both of them had ridden the bicycle to the plantation often, bringing food to the prisoners who lovingly called the ten-year-old »Little Angel«.

When we said good-by, Mrs. Steinbüchler gave me a bag of apples from her garden, and then I met Father Quirmbach again at the place we had agreed upon. We drove to Schleißheim together, but when we were about halfway there, I said, »I would like to rest a little and eat an apple.« Of course I was thinking about the apples which had been given to me. So we got off our bicycles and sat down on the grass; but before I could even take out my apple, my companion handed me one. For a minute I was surprised, but then I took the apple and gave it a hearty bite. »I like your natural manner,« the priest said. »Be sure you stay that way!«

Christl Steinbüchler as a ten-year-old on her way ▷
to the camp

I was completely embarrassed and didn't have the courage to admit that I meant my apple, not his. I had no idea that he had some, too. This little episode is the reason why I remember this trip so well.

One September morning in 1944, I was once again on my usual weekly trip to Dachau. Nearing the camp, I was suddenly overcome by an unexplainable fear. I didn't have the courage to go any farther. Then I saw a little side road. The thought flashed through my mind that I could avoid all the guards and still get to the garden by taking this road. So I turned off the main road. After a while the side road led into a little wood. Summoning up all my courage, I drove on. All of a sudden I was stopped by an SS-guard. Terrified, I got off the bicycle. He barked at me sharply: »Show me your papers!« Then I was even more terrified since I didn't have them with me. I never took them along by design. After thinking for a second; I said resolutely, »I'm not showing my papers. I'd rather turn back,« and tore my bicycle away from him with a jerk. The guard was so stunned by my spontaneous reaction that he did not stop me from going back down the narrow road again.

Over and over again the thought went through my mind: »Why did you really want to take a side road? God is with you!« My fear vanished, I took the usual route, and everything went well. My trust in God was restored.

At the beginning of October I had to go to the Abbey in Metten. Shortly before I left, Sister Saba told me that it had to do with Abbot Korbinian Hofmeister who was also imprisoned in Dachau, but not in the priests' block. He was in the »bunker« with others, not only because of some written papers, but also for sending food packages — as far as I can remember. After breakfast, I headed for the train station, but when I wanted to buy my ticket, I realized that I had forgotten my purse. In my distress, I went to the ticket counter and asked the woman standing behind me if she could lend me three reichsmark for the ticket. After that I made it just in time to the train which took me to Landshut.

While I waited inside for the next train to Deggendorf, the hall filled with people. Clutching their last possessions, they had fled from the Russians and were pushing farther and farther toward the west.

On the train, three young women sat near me. I could tell from their conversation that their husbands were in Russia. One of them said, »We've already lost the war as it is.« The other woman agreed with her. Infuriated, the third woman cried in a voice quivering with rage, »We can't lose the war! The Führer won't allow it because then everything would have been in vain.« Terrified, the other two women looked at me. Dead silence! I was glad when I could get off at Deggendorf.

I stayed with our Sisters in Metten for a little while first, then took care of my business with the Prior at the Benedictine Abbey. He told me that a package for Abbot Korbinian was checked in the baggage room in Landshut. I was to take this along on the way back and deliver it to the Haaser family the next time I went to Dachau. Sister Saba had the exact address. Then the Prior showed me the abbey grounds and church. When I said good-by, he gave me a jar of honey from their own apiary.

Since there was still time, I went back to our Sisters, who were just then picking fruit in their large garden. The local leader gave me a whole sack of beautiful apples. Although they were for Sister Saba, I could eat as many as I wanted on the way. By this time, however, my stomach had become quite delicate and could only tolerate half an apple at most.

Even though all the Sisters were very friendly, I was too afraid to tell them that I had forgotten my purse. While I did have my return ticket, I didn't have a single pfennig when I got on the train, and I needed 40 pfennig to claim the package in Landshut. In this embarrassing situation once again, there was nothing left to do except tell an unknown woman about my need and ask her for 40 pfennig. Friendly and smiling, she helped me out of my distress. When I acknowledged my forgetfulness at home, Sister Saba took my adventure calmly, but I had to take a good scolding from Sister Vigoris.

The next time I went to Dachau, I first looked for the Haaser apartment which I found on the second floor at 1 Weinmann Street. I met a kind and motherly woman in Mrs. Haaser, who already knew that I was coming and said that her daughter Anni would deliver the package to the abbot. Then she told me about her six children, whom I would get to know in time and invited me to a cup of tea while she talked. The warm drink tasted good since the October weather was already cool. During a later visit I also met Mr. Haaser.

One gloomy autumn day I went to deliver some packages to Toni Beer. To my amazement, her behavior had changed noticeably. Instead of chatting with me as she usually did, she only remarked curtly, »My father wants to talk to you.« Full of trepidation, I waited for Mr. Beer. When he came, he ordered me not to make any future deliveries, saying, »I can no longer take the responsibility for my family and for myself that you are delivering packages for the prisoners here. Don't ever set foot in my house again!«

As uncompromising as Mr. Beer was, he did not send me off completely at a loss or without help. He did say that I could leave the food packages for the prisoners at the camp's post office on Eicke Square, and that they were certain to be delivered. Nevertheless, I went away very dejected.

When I came into the shop, I told Father Schönwälder about this conversation. I had the impression that he already knew, since he, too, seemed depressed. But he didn't make any comment whatsoever about my painful experience in the Beer family's apartment. Up to this time it had meant at least a little security for me.

After that I never saw the Beer family or heard anything about them again. Father Schönwälder told me after the war that for purposes of exoneration, he made the statement that Mr. Beer had performed a good deed for the prisoners by his involvement in the »Food Parcel Project«. I am sorry that I never met his daughter again and was never able to thank her for her friendly and loyal help. I heard years later, however, that she had married Canaval, a journalist whom she had met as a prisoner in the Dachau Concentration Camp, but that she had died later.

Father Stanislaus surely knew about the affair with the Beer family, too. To help me, he wrote down the names and numbers of the prisoners to whom I was to address the packages in the future. On my next trip, I delivered the packages at the post office on Eicke Square. Even though my heart was pounding a little, everything went smoothly, and I even found this new solution to be a real relief, because I didn't have to drive past the guards with so many packages any more. Father Stanislaus could also confirm each time if the packages which had been mailed had reached the addressees.

The Extraordinary Assignment

During the first week of Advent, Father Schönwälder told me that he had a very important assignment for me from Father Pies. Then he handed me two unsealed letters from him. One was addressed to Cardinal Faulhaber and the other to Johannes Zawacki, a Jesuit brother. I myself was to read them first before passing them on to the addressees so that I would know precisely what they contained. Then Father Schönwälder told me that Karl Leisner, a deacon who had been imprisoned in the Dachau Concentration Camp for a long time already, was seriously ill in the infirmary. Father Pies looked after him as a friend and sometimes also gave him nursing care.

A French bishop had recently been put into the priests' block. Father Pies, together with Karl Leisner and Bishop Gabriel Piguet, had considered the possibility of the bishop ordaining the terminally ill deacon in the camp chapel. Various things would be needed, however, and the details were given in the two letters. Father Pies had told him that I, accompanied by Brother Johannes, was to deliver the letter to the Cardinal in person. I was to orally confirm Father Pies' written request for the approval of Karl Leisner's ordination, and Brother Johannes could support my statement.

I was to bring the written permission to Dachau the next week for the following reasons: First, it was certain that the bishop would not remain in the priests' block very long, but would soon join the »honorable prisoners« in the bunker, and second, the deacon's state of health was already so bad that nobody dared to believe that he would live to see the liberation of the concentration camp. The assignment that I received with these two letters made a deep impression on me.

Before I started home, Father Schönwälder also gave me a large Advent wreath for the Sisters at Saint Clara's and a small one for myself, both of them gifts from the prisoners as a sign of their gratitude. After I had the »SS-Road« behind me, I got off the bicycle. It had begun to snow softly and I wanted to walk part of the way and gather my thoughts. An almost indescribably deep feeling of happiness welled up within me over having just received such a noble assignment. It was Advent, a special time since my childhood, and the prisoners had lovingly made up a little Advent wreath as a gift for me.

When I arrived at home, I read the two letters with Sister Saba and Sister Vigoris. Then I sealed them, hoping that they would safely reach the addressees. I put the letter for Brother Johannes Zawacki, the Jesuit in Pullach, into a mailbox downtown and carefully kept the one for Cardinal Faulhaber.

Brother Johannes visited us during the second week of Advent. He had already visited Brother Erich briefly a few times during the summer, so Saint Clara's and the Sisters were not unknown to him, but I knew him only in passing. We went to Munich together. The Jesuits from Pullach had previously announced our arrival at the archepiscopal residence,

Michael Cardinal Faulhaber ▷

82

Johannes Zawacki, SJ

Otto Pies, SJ, with Deacon Karl Leisner

and Father Hubert Wagner, the cardinal's secretary, was waiting for us. He took us into a sumptuously decorated baroque room, where I handed him the letter. He took it to the Cardinal immediately. After a short time, he returned with the Cardinal, who gave us a warm welcome and asked for our names and occupations. He wanted to know how I had come to the plantation in the first place, and let me talk for a long time. Now and then he would ask me a question, wanting to hear further details about my experiences. The conversation lasted about an hour. At the end, the Cardinal said that we should wait a little while and then he left with his secretary. Both returned about 30 minutes later, and the Cardinal handed me a letter containing the permission for the ordination. The secretary had brought the holy oils, the necessary ritual books, and a stole. Then the Cardinal gave us very serious instructions about keeping strict silence about this matter. After the ordination I was to bring credible documentation and the articles which I had just received back to the archepiscopal residence.

At the beginning of our meeting, the Cardinal seemed very reserved, but during the course of our conversation he became more receptive and addressed me by my first name, calling me »Josefine« instead of »Josefa«, however. He gave us his blessing before cordially dismissing us. Brother Johannes returned to Pullach.[4]

During that same week and on the prearranged day, I brought the crucial letter and the necessary articles for the ordination to Dachau. Under some pretext or another, Father Pies came to see Father Schönwälder in the shop, wanting to know as soon as possible how our dialogue with Cardinal Faulhaber had gone and whether I had brought the important documents. To his great joy, I could give him everything. He then told me that the ordination would be on the coming Sunday, Gaudete Sunday, the 17th of December.

Father Karl Leisner celebrated Eucharist for the first time in the camp chapel on the feast of St. Stephen, December 26th.[5] On the 27th, I was again in Dachau. Father Schönwälder gave me the documentation for the ordination and those articles necessary for the

[4] See Appendix
[5] See Appendix

administration of the sacrament which I had received from Cardinal Faulhaber with the request to bring everything back again.

This time Father Quirmbach accompanied me to the camp and used the opportunity to personally deliver packages to his Pallottine brothers. It was no longer possible to send them, since many train stations had been bombed and the trains would often be strafed by low flying enemy aircraft. Having arrived in Schleißheim on the way home, we had to watch for the next passenger train to Freising. Scheduled transportation was already a thing of the past. There was only a little snow on the ground, and it wasn't very cold. After leaning our bicycles against the gate, we began our wait. I wanted to be alone with my thoughts, so I didn't carry on any conversation. I told Father Quirmbach that he could feel free to go into the waiting room while I would watch the bicycles and call him when the train came. I was totally taken up with what the prisoners had enthusiastically told me about Karl Leisner's ordination and celebration of Eucharist for the first time. Leaning on the wooden railing, I was lost in thought, so while I did see a train come in, I didn't come to until only a few minutes later when it pulled off. Then the thought flashed through my mind — it's going toward Freising! I ran into the waiting room and cried, »The train is leaving!« When Father Quirmbach came, all we could see was the back of the last car. My companion was appalled and I was completely overcome with remorse. It could be hours before another train came, so Father neither trusted my vigilance nor wanted to go into the waiting room any more. However, we were very lucky because about an hour later another train stopped which did take us to Freising.

Azaleas For My Parents

At Christmas, my mother sent me a package which also contained a letter from my father. He had written that various persons had told him that they had met me on the way to or from Dachau. Until this time, my parents always thought that I was well taken care of by the Sisters in Freising, but now they had to hear repeatedly that I was apparently away a lot. They were concerned and wanted me to explain why the word »Dachau« always came up in the conversation.

I talked about this letter with Sister Vigoris, who thought that it would be better not to answer in writing. She and Sister Saba would consider the possibility of my spending two weeks at home in January. Shortly after New Year's, I went to the plantation in Dachau once more, where I said that I would be taking two weeks' vacation at home with my parents. On my way back, I would stop there again. The prisoners, wanting to give my parents some happiness, gave me four pink azalea plants to take to them, a moving gesture from these poor men. Until then I had hardly ever seen azaleas with such beautiful blossoms, and I was enormously happy to be able to surprise my parents with them. After visiting the camp, I left my bicycle at the Steinbüchler's and took the passenger train through Ingolstadt and on to Adelschlag, Möckenlohe's train station. It was already dark when I came home. My mother was overcome with surprise and joy — her eyes were filled with tears.

This first evening I was alone with my parents. My sister, five years older than I, lived with her little boy in Eichstätt — her husband was a medical orderly in Russia. My brother, three years younger than I, was in the Labor Service. After supper I knew my parents were waiting to hear about my trips to Dachau, so I brought up the topic myself. Although they grew frightened and noticeably concerned about me, they still made every effort to understand — yes, even more! In the end, they were in agreement with what I was doing and I got the impression that my father especially not only approved of my trips to Dachau, but was even proud of me. It was clearly a satisfaction for him that I was allowed to go and actually did. Indeed, he himself had always suffered because he had had to hold back his aversion for the regime and could not express his disapproval more openly.

One day in the summer of 1942 I was at home on vacation and met the mayor. He started talking with me and, in the course of the conversation, advised me to convince my father not to express his political views as openly as he was doing. The man basically meant well; his youngest daughter was a candidate like I was with the School Sisters. At heart, he probably had the same views as almost everyone else in the village, but he was in a very difficult position by reason of his office. He went on to say that he would really have had to report my father many times already, but he wanted to avoid having to do that. Nevertheless, my father absolutely had to hold back more.

This conversation made little impression on me at the time since I held the exact same political views as my father. So while I did tell him about our conversation at home, I did it very objectively because I did not want to influence my father in any way. I wasn't afraid for him either because, as an 11 or 12-year-old, I had had a crucial experience which had given me assurance that a respectable citizen of the village could not be simply denounced, arrested and imprisoned just because of a negative political statement.

It was the summer of 1935 or 1936. I had driven to Ochsenfeld with my bicycle to visit my confirmation sponsor, as I had often done before. Resi, her daughter, was especially happy when I came. She was a few years older than I and liked to tell about her experiences. This time Resi had an especially exciting story to tell me. A short time before, Father Willibald Heimloth, the pastor in the village, had been arrested by the Nazis and taken to Eichstätt. Apparently he had railed against euthanasia from the pulpit. Even though I didn't know what the word meant, it was enough for me to know that it had to do with something against Hitler.

We stood at the bakery counter while she told me her story. Whenever someone would come in, Resi would quickly wait on the customer so she could immediately continue where she left off. She almost glowed with excitement and enthusiasm as she described in great detail how the village folk reacted to the pastor's arrest. The whole village was astir, no one pursued the usual occupations, all were openly outraged over what had happened. A delegation of men immediately drove to Eichstätt to bring their pastor home again. Once in Eichstätt, they wouldn't calm down or take no for an answer until they had the definite promise that the pastor could come home again soon. That really did happen. For a long time after that, groups of men took turns guarding the parish property day and night so their pastor could not be taken away again.

Since we had an open view of the church and parish house through the store window, Resi's account was especially vivid.

This story made me certain that a united village community can protect and save an individual who is being threatened. This inner security kept me from worrying about my father.

It was a very beautiful two weeks' vacation with my parents, but not without shadows. Stefan, my cousin, was killed in action. He was the second son his parents had lost in the war and now their oldest son was the only one left. This death was also very painful for me, since I had been very close to my cousins when we were in school together. The Requiem was celebrated for Stefan during my vacation. My mother placed the four azalea plants on the catafalque. After the funeral liturgy, we gave two of them to Stefan's mother, who was my aunt and baptismal sponsor. Thus the azaleas from the camp in Dachau took on another special meaning for me and became a symbol of how closely joy and suffering are bound together in life.

My mother spoiled me during these two weeks — at least as much as she could during the war. It was truly good for me, helping me to relax a little from the strain of the past months and gather new strength for the difficult weeks which were sure to come.

The evening before I left, Mother packed a large parcel of food for the prisoners. She wanted very much to return the happiness which they had given her. Because we ran a small farm, it was easier for us to give away bread, butter, sausage and smoked meat. Saying good-by was especially hard on my mother. She went with me to the station and before I got on the train, she pleaded with me to be careful.

When I arrived at Dachau, I went to the Steinbüchlers first to pick up my bicycle. I had also brought some food for Mrs. Steinbüchler and for Mrs. Haaser, which made both families very happy, since these things were very scarce at the time. Then I drove to the post office on Eicke Square and mailed the package for the camp. I was able to give a present to Father Schönwälder and Father Stanislaus from the things my mother had packed for me. They were very grateful and told me that the prisoners had become very depressed during the past two weeks when I didn't come to the plantation. Each day the hunger became more severe and typhoid fever was rampant. The prisoners had been counting on an imminent liberation already during the summer of 1944 and had hoped to be home for Christmas. But now there was no prospect in sight that the war would end soon. These gloomy impressions weighed heavily on my heart, and I went back to Freising in very low spirits.

Winter Sets In
Typhoid Fever Epidemic in the Camp

While I was away, a large amount of food had been gathered at Saint Clara's for the prisoners. Whatever food the Sisters had received from their families for Christmas was set aside for Dachau. Sister Vigoris and I packed several food parcels, and a package had also been left for me to deliver to the Abbot from Metten.

Winter had set in with all its severity in the meantime. It was freezing cold and there was much snow. Because the streets in Freising were open, I didn't worry about the rest of the trip, but when I came to the road in Schleißheim which would take me to Dachau, I realized, to my horror, that it wasn't cleared.

It must have been used by a few vehicles, however, since there were deep tracks in the snowbanks. I tried to get on my bicycle several times, but always in vain.

Meanwhile it had begun to snow again, and in the end there was nothing left for me to do but walk the ten kilometers and push my heavily loaded bicycle — an extremely wearisome task.

It was already past noontime when I arrived at the Haaser's, sweating and frozen stiff at the same time. The good woman was appalled at the way I looked with my eyebrows and hair covered with heavy frost. She made me take off my boots and everything else that was wet so they could be hung up to dry right away. Very sympathetic, she made me some tea and the hot drink was good. When Maria, her daughter, came with her four-year-old for a visit, Mrs. Haaser immediately told her about my strenuous journey. Maria suggested that I load the packages on her child's sled and pull them to the plantation. That would make the trip easier for me.

After I had recovered a little from my exhaustion, we loaded up the sled, which I pulled to the post office on Eicke Square and then on to

Father Schönwälder. Our short conversation, as well as that with Father Stanislaus, made me very depressed once again. I had to hear that hardly any more packages were coming into the camp because more and more railroad lines were disrupted. Besides that, typhoid fever was spreading throughout the camp. I said a very sorrowful good-by, brought the sled back to the Haasers and started the weary journey home. At least the bicycle wasn't as heavily laden as it was that morning, since the tea which I had bought didn't weigh nearly as much as the food and medicine had. Fortunately, I could still catch the train in Schleißheim for Freising, where the Sisters were already worried about me. I told them that I had to walk the whole distance and would like to take a sled for the entire trip next time.

I also told the Sisters how hunger and typhoid fever were getting worse and worse in the camp and how I was haunted again by the prisoners' pleas for medicine to counteract the epidemic. During the following days, Sister Vigoris went to the pharmacists she knew, confidentially asking for the necessary medicine. She was known and appreciated by the local businesses, because she was responsible for the financial concerns of the homes for the children and for the elderly as well as for the farm at Saint Clara's — duties which she fulfilled with great prudence. For this reason she was able to procure medicine for Dachau again and again.

Although Sister Saba always went along with her, she wasn't able to conceal a certain scepticism about the relief action. I can still hear her saying with great sadness, »All our efforts are only a drop in the bucket!« But I believed that this drop in the bucket would help save the lives of many prisoners.

In spite of the bad weather and poor road conditions, I went to Dachau once again that same week. This time Sister Vigoris and I loaded up a sled and then I started off, but going the long way from Schleißheim to Dachau with a heavily loaded sled demanded almost as much energy as taking the bicycle. The entire strain was offset, however, by my being able to bring much joy into the camp once more.

Once again it was already dark as I wearily dragged the sled from the train station to Saint Clara's. I met the Cardinal's secretary on the way and whispered to him, »I just came from Dachau.« We didn't say anything else. When

Sister Vigoris noticed how terribly exhausted I was, she decided to send Maria with me in the future. This candidate did come with me a few times.

Cardinal Faulhaber had moved to Cathedral Hill (Domberg) in Freising because of the heavy bombing raids on Munich during December and January. Mother M. Almeda, our General Superior, arranged for me to have an audience with him in late January. I returned the written documentation of Karl Leisner's ordination, the ritual books and the stole. This visit was completely different from the earlier one in Munich because the Cardinal already knew me and I was able to sense his trust from the very beginning.

During the interview, the Cardinal was eager to know what I had experienced and what I had learned from the prisoners' accounts. During our conversation, he called me a »Tarcisia[6] of our times« and asked me whether I could really keep still. Surprised, I looked at him and said with conviction that I could certainly

7 See Appendix

manage to do that. His answer was a gentle reproach, however spoken with kindness and fatherliness: »But you told my secretary on the street that you were coming from Dachau!« He gave me his blessing as I left and also made an energetic sign of the cross on my lips, praying that I be able to keep silence during this dangerous time.

The next time I went to Dachau, I told Father Schönwälder and Father Stanislaus about this visit with Cardinal Faulhaber, mentioning, too, that he had called me »Tarcisia« once during the course of the conversation. Father Stanislaus, who had been thinking about a suitable religious name for me for a long time already, was enthusiastic and thought I had to be given this name when I was received into the congregation, a wish which nevertheless remained unfulfilled. Besides, there was no thought of reception at the time because the political situation was worsening from week to week. Even the people in Freising had to go to the shelters almost every night because of the threat of air raids. At the time, I was responsible for ten to twelve boys, ages three to six, who had to be awakened from sleep, brought to the

basement and put to bed again on cots —
sometimes with bitter tears.

While the longing for the end of the war
mounted increasingly among the people, it
became almost unbearable among the
prisoners. Almost every time that I went to
Dachau, I would go to the pepper mill and
speak with the workers there after I saw Father
Schönwälder. They were living solely on the
hope that the liberation would have to be
coming very soon.

It was often very wet and rainy, gloomy and
unpleasantly cool. The weather dampened the
mood in general, but its effect in the camp was
especially bad. Each day many prisoners died.
Father Pies and Father Schönwälder asked me
for the Holy Oils so they could administer the
Sacrament of the Anointing to the dying. I got
them from the Cardinal's secretary at the
Domberg in Freising, thus making it possible
for many to have one last consolation.

The news from the fronts became more
depressing each day, but banners with the
words, »We want total war!« and other similar
rallying cries were still hanging on the
Domberg Wall. They were already faded and
torn, but nobody took them down. Nor were

they able to shake the passersby out of their dull apathy and weary despair.

Seeing My Brother for the Last Time

During the last days of February, my brother surprised me with a visit. He had been dismissed from the Labor Service and was to wait for his summons to military service. The happiness on both sides was great since we had not seen each other for a long time and my brother wanted to stay with me for a few days. We visited the cathedral and walked through the city that same afternoon, but when we came home, a telegram from our father was waiting for us with the message that Josef should return home immediately. He was to report for duty in two days.

That evening was all that we had left for saying good-by. We had been very close ever since childhood and now awful premonitions were weighing heavily upon us. The next morning, I accompanied my brother to the train station. Josef stood sadly at the open compartment window and I looked up to him sadly. We shook hands once again and I ran a little way alongside the moving train. Then we waved to each other one last time. I went back to Saint Clara's alone and with a heavy heart. Indeed, we were never to see each other again.

At the end of March, I met my father very unexpectedly at the train station in Freising one day and was appalled by his sad expression. Depressed, he shook my hand, but there wasn't the least bit of joy on seeing me again. At first he only said that he wanted to go back to Saint Clara's with me. On the way he told me that my aunt, Sister Stanislava, had telephoned from Lenggreis, saying that Josef would be assigned in the West soon. So he had gone to Lenggreis with food, hoping to see his boy once more. He arrived there, but never met him. Josef's division had already started out. Now he wanted to visit me and told me that I should take the food to the prisoners on my next trip. My father and I were filled with the gloomy premonition that we would never see Josef again. Already on April eighth, my brother was killed in action in Württemberg. He was barely 18 years old. The painful news reached my parents shortly before Pentecost and I heard it only at the beginning of June.

Signs of Dissolution

By the middle of February, the snow had melted enough so that I could go by bicycle again. It was the only bicycle that belonged to Saint Clara's and was used by all the girls in the house. Almost as if by a miracle, I had never had any trouble with it. The tires were already worn down, the bicycle itself wasn't in the best condition anymore and spare parts were not to be had. One day I had bad luck. I had already gone to Eicke Square to deliver my packages and was on the way to the plantation. Then I heard a short, high-pitched whistle — I had a flat tire! Dejected, I pushed my bicycle to the market garden and could already see myself walking the whole way back to Schleißheim, pushing the broken bicycle alongside of me. Max, the Polish boy who was always on the road when I was expected, recognized my misfortune as soon as he saw me. Filled with joy, he cried, »I can fix that, Miss!« and took the bicycle from me.

When I came out of the shop, the young man was already standing in front of the door with the repaired bicycle, his whole face beaming. He was overjoyed that for once he didn't just get something from me, but, in return for the eagerly awaited bread which I would bring him, could also do something for me. He had found the necessary material to patch the tire in the bag attached to the bicycle. From this day on, Max thoroughly checked my bicycle every time that I came.

I had another happy experience during my journeys in March. From time to time, Mr. Gaster would give me some pink and white primroses to take along for our chapel. He had raised them himself. The last flowers which I brought home from the plantation decorated our »Holy Sepulcher« on Good Friday.

One morning in March I was surprised to find Brother Erich waiting for me with another Jesuit, Brother Bernhard Gluth, whom I had never met before. He had come to Bavaria with the stream of refugees from Silesia. Brother Erich requested temporary housing at Saint Clara's for Brother Bernhard and himself. Filled with urgent concern, he asked me what news I had from Dachau and how Father Pies was. I told him about the situation there — the hunger had become unbearable, typhoid fever was raging dreadfully, and the prisoners could hardly wait any longer for the end of their suffering.

At the end of March, Father Schönwälder told me that there was great excitement in the camp. Some days before, smaller groups of German priests had been discharged. It was a happy surprise for some — for others, painful disappointment. Some of Father Eichten's brother Redemptorists were among the fortunate ones. They came to us in Freising and I was permitted to share in their unexpected reunion with our chaplain. The mutual happiness was overwhelming.

Sister Saba gave temporary housing to many discharged prisoners, mainly priests from the Diocese of Münster. I still remember one of them, Father Reinhold Friedrichs, very well. There were also some priests from the Austrian dioceses. Sometimes eight to ten men would be staying at our house. As soon as they had a chance to go home, they took leave of us, full of gratitude. Other prisoners were housed as guests of the Vincentian Sisters, the place where Father Quirmbach worked.

After the war was over, however, some »black sheep« slipped in. I still remember one such swindler very well. He was supposed to have come from a concentration camp — not from Dachau — and told us some gruesome things. Some people believed him since, in the meantime, very much about the cruelty in the camps had been revealed. One day, however, the man was picked up by the police, and we found out that everything he told us was made up.

My trips to Dachau were also becoming ever more dangerous since low flying aircraft were shooting at the trains more and more. At the beginning of April, Sister Saba, Sister Vigoris and I considered once again if it might be better to ride the bicycle all the way to Dachau and take a companion along. Brother Bernhard Gluth, SJ, was very willing to go with me. When we started out on April 18th, it was still relatively quiet on the streets. We were able to deliver our packages as usual at Eicke Square and take care of our business with Father Schönwälder and in the pepper mill. This time we could even go through the whole plantation —

somehow everything seemed to be in the process of breaking up. After this strenuous journey, we rested a while at the Steinbüchler's, where we didn't talk about anything else except the end of the war and the expected liberation of the camp.

On the way home, we rode our bicycles down another road since we wanted to make two short stops on the way. As we turned on to the country road, a heavy bomber suddenly flew over us. Seeing the direction it was going, I cried in terror, »They're flying over Freising!« Brother Bernhard couldn't calm me down. We soon heard the muffled detonations. We had been chatting excitedly before that — now I became completely silent. I was afraid for Freising and its inhabitants, afraid for Saint Clara's, for the children, for the Sisters. I was almost strangled by fear.

While still on the road, we heard that Freising really had been hit in the bombing raid. Coming closer to the city, we saw that the area around the train station was destroyed. Thanks be to God, there were only broken windows at Saint Clara's, which was situated about 15–20 minutes from the train station. The whole city was paralyzed with horror and grief.

Nevertheless, I drove the bicycle to the camp once more between the 18th and the 28th of April, this time accompanied by Father Quirmbach. He was very nervous and told me about the bombing raid on April 18th, a raid which he had survived in the Vincentian Sisters' basement. Most of the building had been destroyed by a volley of bombs. His own life and the lives of all in the house were in the greatest danger during this attack. I could understand why he was so extremely nervous.

On the street, everything gradually turned into complete chaos, the likes of which I had never seen before. People with their last possessions packed into baby buggies and little handcarts, onto bicycles and wheelbarrows, surged from the northeast toward the southwest in jumbled confusion. Even soldiers were in the crowd. »In such circumstances, it would really be irresponsible for a girl to travel alone by bicycle,« Father Quirmbach maintained. Apparently he had asked Sister Saba if he could accompany me.

In spite of everything we did have a good trip to Dachau and could even deliver our packages. After that we went to Father Schönwälder and took care of our secret business.

Both there and in the pepper mill, we again met many prisoners known to both of us. It was the last time that we met in the camp. There was an indescribable commotion everywhere. When we were still at the plantation, the air raid sirens went off. In a flash, all the prisoners were gone. We let go of our bicycles and threw ourselves to the ground. Bombers thundered over us. We escaped, but were completely terrified. On the way home, everything looked the same as it did on our trip out, and we arrived in Freising, exhausted but grateful that we had gotten through the day without a scratch.

Going to the Camp For the Last Time
Meeting the Death March

Father Schönwälder and I had agreed that I would come again on April 28th, even though there was no way of knowing if that would even be possible. I was not well-informed about how far the front had already advanced. The Sisters

◁ *Column of Marching Prisoners*

had great reservations about letting me go once more, but I felt an obligation to go since I had made the promise to come.

On the evening of the 27th, I asked Sister Vigoris to help me pack all the food that we could spare. We had asked Brother Erich to go with me, but when we started out, I could see that he really did not want to go along since there were already gloomy signs of defeat and dissolution in Freising. He told me that he wanted to hear the latest radio reports first, so we went into a house on Market Square. Just to be safe, we took the bicycles into the hallway. In the living room, we met Brother Bernhard standing with the family in front of the radio. I was kept in terrible suspense by what we were hearing. There were repeated announcements that the station had been occupied by the »Bavarian Liberation Front«. I was fascinated by this piece of news. As the liberators spoke, we could repeatedly hear other voices coming through, talking about »traitors«. It was terribly exciting. Until then it had been forbidden under threat of severe punishment to turn on such a station — but I had the greatest aversion for the official news.

Ever since Hitler had taken over in 1933, the radio was used by the National Socialists for propaganda purposes, being especially directed at the young people, even children. Once when I was in the third grade, all the school children had been taken to a restaurant to hear a broadcast of a talk by Hitler. That meant sitting still and having to listen to a harsh voice screaming uninterruptedly for more than an hour. It was dreadful because I liked to move about a lot. Besides that, while I could barely understand a word of what was being said, my ears were ringing from the shouting. The whole thing was a nightmare.

During the course of the following years we had to go to the restaurant and listen to Hitler giving his talks several times. Once we listened to Hitler when the Saarland was being returned to Germany in 1935. At the end of the talk, we all ran through the village, yelling and screaming. Our elderly neighbor called me to her garden fence and asked why we were making such a dreadful noise. I replied, »Germany got back the Saarland!« It probably wasn't this news that had set off our howling and screaming. It was a simple reaction at having to sit still and listen so long.

Back to April 28th, 1945: I could hardly believe that something so positive as the

appeals of the »Bavarian Liberation Front«
could come out of a radio set. We must have
stood in front of the radio for an hour, listening
to the most contradictory news reports. Then
Brother Erich was even less willing to go with
me to Dachau, but I absolutely had to go once
more and see with my own eyes how the
prisoners were. Therefore I put such pressure
on him that he decided to go with me.

The stream of refugees on the country road
had swollen immensely. Once in Dachau, we
asked Mrs. Steinbüchler what she knew about
the camp. She told us that no one from her
family had been at the market garden since
Brother Bernhard and I had been there. The
tension in the entire village was enormous,
with everyone feverishly waiting for the Americans to arrive from Ingolstadt to free the
prisoners.

We drove on into the camp. The SS-Road
was quiet and desolate. Even the SS-family
homes looked as if they were deserted. Eicke
Square gave the same impression. The post office was closed without any explanation on the
door. We slowly drove along the wall and plantation. Nowhere was there a guard to be seen.
This was almost more eerie than seeing the

usual sentries. Father Schönwälder wasn't there either, and the shop was closed. On the other side, the administration building was just as deserted as the SS-residences.

We turned around and pushed our bicycles along the wall once more. Then we discovered an open door. We carefully approached it, looked inside and saw the barracks in front of us. While we were standing there, having no idea what to do, a prisoner came out of the background. He turned to us shyly and asked in broken German what we wanted. We told him that we wanted to deliver packages at the Eicke Post Office and see Mr. Schönwälder in the shop, but we were met with closed doors everywhere. As we were talking, some more prisoners approached us, all foreigners of various nationalities. They thought that Father Schönwälder had probably gone into hiding like many others who still wanted to be freed. A large segment of the prisoners had been driven off to the south that morning. They themselves had gone into hiding, too, wanting to escape this transport which they were sure would end in death. We gave these prisoners the packages which they accepted with great joy and gratitude. Then we left the desolate grounds.

Because I wanted to see Mrs. Haaser again, I asked Brother Erich to go with me. While he did comply with my wish, he did not accompany me into the apartment. I wanted to hurry in and out, but it wasn't as simple as that. Mrs. Haaser was very happy that I had come and urged me to have a cup of tea with her, so my visit lasted somewhat longer. It was the last time that I saw Mrs. Haaser. Seeing Brother Erich again, I noticed his impatience. I apologized and explained that I did not want to hurt Mrs. Haaser after all the good she had done for me that whole winter. He replied tersely, »A man, a word — a woman, a dictionary!« I had to laugh aloud, but it dissolved the minor discord between us and we started home.

We drove along the country road from Dachau to Freising for the last time. Suddenly, far ahead in the distance, we saw a long, dark band pushing ahead very slowly. Horrified, I asked Brother Erich, »Are those ahead of us the prisoners who were driven south?« We drove farther and came closer and closer to this somber procession that seemed almost endless. Finally we could distinguish human beings, pitiable destitutes with dirty grey blankets wrapped around them. SS-guards, holding whips, were walking to the left and to the right of the prisoners, who looked like old men ready to collapse, even though most of them must have been middle-aged or younger. Again and again someone would try to pull out of the line and exhausted, drop into the ditch, or they would simply collapse right there in the ranks. The SS-men brutally forced these poor people to stand up and, kicking and hitting them, pushed them back in line. Whips lashing, they drove the emaciated figures forward. We got off our bicycles.

In desperation, I asked myself, »Where are the prisoners supposed to go? Where are they supposed to stay during the night? It's already late afternoon.« I broke down at the sight of this massive wretchedness and bending over the handlebars on my bicycle, cried unrestrainedly. After a while Brother Erich screamed at me, »Let's go! There isn't a thing that we can do.« He was right. I pulled myself together, and we pushed our bicycles past the long column of misery. God alone knows the number of Dachau prisoners who were yet to die as a result of this dreadfully insane action.

I hardly noticed anything else the rest of the way home. All I could see was the column of prisoners in front of me. This image of atrocity has been painfully burned into my very being.

The next day, the 29th of April, Dachau was captured by American troops and the concentration camp was liberated without any German resistance.

Despite futile Nazi resistance, Freising was also occupied on April 30th.

Then there were new problems which demanded all our attention and energy, but I continued to worry about the fate of the former prisoners. The Jesuit brothers told me later that even though many died on the death march, many were also able to be saved.

People Who Meant Very Much To Me

As the years went on, the relationships I had formed with the men and women whom I had come to know during my »Dachau Year« became less close. However, I can tell a little about the later life of those whom I got to know especially well and about those who gave me special assistance on my trips to Dachau. Although they have already appeared in my story, it seems good to give a brief biographical summary for each of them.

Dr. Ferdinand Schönwälder

Father Schönwälder came to Saint Clara's quite unexpectedly a few weeks after Freising had surrendered to the Americans. It was a very joyful and moving experience for all of us that he could visit us as a free man. Sister Saba, Sister Vigoris and I sat down together with Father Schönwälder for a long time and we had him tell us about his last experiences in the

Dr. Ferdinand Schönwälder

120

camp and its liberation by the Americans on April 29th. We returned the notes he had written on loose sheets of paper and which he had entrusted to me, one by one, during my trips.

Later on, Father Schönwälder visited us at Saint Clara's another two or three times. During August I was preparing for reception, which took place in the parish church in Weichs on August 28, 1945. I had invited Father Schönwälder to this celebration, and he came, accompanied by Mrs. Steinbüchler and her daughter, Christl, the »Angel from Dachau«. They brought me a beautiful bouquet of white lilies and yellow roses. Christl wore her white First Communion dress and had memorized a poem for me. On this occasion it made Father Schönwälder very happy to meet my parents. He even visited my home once.

Father Schönwälder also came to my first profession on August 29, 1946, once again accompanied by Mrs. Steinbüchler and Christl.

At the end of March, 1947, he visited me in Garmisch where I was then missioned, and again after 1948, at Mariahilf Square in Munich, where I was able to complete my training as a needlework teacher. That was the last time I saw Father Schönwälder. Even though he would occasionally write to me, send me magazines with articles he had published every now and then, and send me personal greetings, contacts became fewer and fewer. From 1958 on, Father Schönwälder was pastor in Gundihausen near Landshut.

Elisabeth and Wilhelm Haas, sister and brother-in-law of Karl Leisner, repeatedly expressed their desire to take me with them on a trip to Gundihausen, since they wanted to talk together with us about the time Father Schönwälder and Karl were together in Dachau. Unfortunately, we repeatedly postponed this visit for lack of time until it was too late. Father Schönwälder died in March, 1980.

In the spring of 1986, some women from Gundihausen invited me to come and tell them about the time their former pastor had been in prison. On this occasion I stood at Father Schönwälder's grave for the first time. This brought back memories of the times we met between May, 1944, and the end of April, 1945. My prayer for him was filled with gratitude for all he had done — under the constant threat of a death sentence — to help his companion prisoners in the plantation. God will reward him for everything.

Stanislaus Wolak, OFM, CAP

During the weeks after the collapse of Germany in May, 1945, I often wondered whether Father Stanislaus had survived the liberation and if so, how. Then one day an American truck drove into the courtyard at St. Clara's. I can still see Father Stanislaus standing on the trailer in front of me, waving happily. Laughing and in great spirits, he jumped down and excused himself for not letting us hear from him for such a long time. Until then he hadn't found any occasion to leave the camp in order to come to Freising with the Americans.

Sister Saba, Sister Vigoris and I had him tell us about his experiences during the previous weeks. Overjoyed at his liberation and filled with youthful enthusiasm, he told us about his plans to emigrate to Australia. He promised to come back again soon or at least to let us hear from him. But it was the last time we saw each other and I never heard from him again. After my novitiate, I repeatedly tried to find out something about Father Stanislaus through Father Schönwälder, but always in vain.

We received the following information as a result of inquiries from the Capuchins only recently: Father Stanislaus Wolak was born in Rozwadow on November 8, 1913, entered the Capuchins and was a member of the Cracow Province. He was probably ordained in May, 1940, but by June of the same year he had already been arrested and taken to the concentration camp in Auschwitz. From there he was transported to Dachau in December, 1940.

The Capuchins told us that after his liberation in 1945, he emigrated to Australia to minister to the Polish immigrants as a beloved pastor who was held in high regard. He died in 1973.

I feel very bad that I never heard anything directly from Father Stanislaus, because after Father Schönwälder and Father Pies, he was the most helpful of the prisoners whom I knew. He shall always be remembered.

Otto Pies, SJ

At the end of May or the beginning of June, 1945, Father Pies, accompanied by Father Friedrich Pfanzelt, the pastor in Dachau, drove

Otto Pies, SJ

a rickety car into Saint Clara's, surprising all of us. They wanted to meet Sister Saba and Sister Vigoris and thank them for all the good which they had done for the prisoners in Dachau. Father Pies told about life in the camp and the work in the market garden. The conversation then turned from the Dachau complex to the evils of National Socialism. He ended with the question, »How could it possibly come to that in Germany?«

That opened up a new realization for me. While I had a happy childhood and was sheltered in my youth, my perspective of everything which was happening as a result of National Socialism was relatively narrow, and I knew much too little about the full scope of this terrible ideology and nothing at all of its criminal proportion. I felt a burning desire to learn at least a little more. The more I heard and read about the atrocities of these twelve years, the deeper my grief became and the more I buried my own memories within.

When I reflect on my journeys to Dachau, this visit with Father Pies made me especially happy. During that difficult year, he had been a great help to me from the very first moment that I met him in Father Schönwälder's shop in the market garden. Even though he was a prisoner himself, his personality radiated a great inner security, and this awakened trust. Every time I was at Dachau, he would come into the shop under some pretense or other whenever possible. It was a profound experience for me to be able to see him now in a free setting. The Sisters, too, were happy to meet in person the priest about whom I had told them so much and to receive his expression of gratitude.

Father Pies told us in great detail how he, with the help of Father Pfanzelt, the parish priest, and some other Jesuits, had managed to get his friend, Karl Leisner, out of the camp and into the sanatorium in Planegg. With joy he also told us how he had been taken in and cared for so well by the Sisters of Mercy. Unfortunately, I never had the pleasure of meeting Karl Leisner in person for various reasons. Ever since I had delivered Cardinal Faulhaber's written permission and the articles necessary for his ordination, I felt especially close to this prisoner in Dachau. While I was in the Novitiate, I learned of his death on August 12, 1945. Around Christmas, 1945, I received a letter from Father Pies with the request that I record my memories of the journeys to the plantation in Dachau. I learned later that it was Wilhelm Leisner, Karl's younger brother, who had expressed this wish to Father Pies. I became very frightened, but at the time it was impossible for me to speak with anyone about my experiences, to say nothing of writing about them. I was still too deeply affected and wounded, could not deal with my memories yet, and had not gained the necessary distance from them. So this wish remained unfulfilled at first.

Then at the beginning of January, 1946, Father Pies turned to Mother M. Almeda Schricker, our General Superior, and asked her to persuade me to record my memories of Dachau. Even though I didn't want to, I complied with her request and wrote a brief account of my experiences. Father Pies put this report in his book, »Stephanus heute. Karl Leisner, Priester und Opfer« (THE VICTORY OF FATHER KARL), published by Butzon & Becker around 1950. In the English translation, my account is on pages 152–164. During the following years when I would be asked to tell something about my trips to Dachau, I would always simply refer to this book about Karl Leisner.

Sometime in the late fifties, Father Pies also published my remembrances together with reports about other women who had done much good for the prisoners in Dachau under similar difficult circumstances. This pamphlet was entitled, »Giving Hands: Women Who Brought Help to Priests in the Concentration Camps« (»Schenkende Hände. Helferinnen der KZ-Priester«) and could be found in the pamphlet racks in many churches. However, the book and the pamphlet have been out of print for years.

Later Father Pies visited me a few more times in Munich-Au. Each of these visits was a great joy for me, and our conversations meant more to me than any other spiritual direction at that time. Father Pies died in a hospital in Mainz on July 1, 1960, and was buried in Münster. He was only 59 years old when he died. My memories of Father Pies became especially vivid in 1987 when Rita Strothjohann, a journalist and photographer, brought me a series of tapes with stories told by priests who had been imprisoned in the concentration camps. Almost all of them mentioned the blessed work of this priest in Dachau and every one of these presented Father Pies just as I had known him and remember him now. It makes me very happy that these priests would have so

Erich Berschtl, SJ

completely confirmed my own high regard for this man after so many years.

Erich Berschtl, SJ

The memories of my trips to Dachau with Brother Erich Berschtl are still vivid because of our stimulating discussions. After I had told him, for example, that I would like to become a School Sister and begin my novitiate, he gave me valuable tips for this time of preparation. He himself had already made his novitiate under the direction of Father Pies.

Brother Erich also told me about his dearly loved home and family in Silesia and could describe its special dish, »Silesian heaven«, to the last detail, including the ingredients and how it was made. His humorous and exciting stories brought me so close to his homeland that I, too, learned to love Silesia.

Our relationship could be described better as a camaraderie. Being older than I (born in 1919) and more educated (having completed the university entrance exams and philosophy studies), his reaction to my spontaneous questions and opinions was sometimes tinged with irony, an irony, however, which never hurt. In September, 1944, he went to Maria Eck to study theology, but returned once more to Freising in March, 1945. Exactly two years later, Sister Vigoris gave me the sad news that Brother Erich had died from the flu in the Jesuit college in Pullach. It was incomprehensible. The war and its life-threatening danger had been over two years before. Now this young cleric had to die from an illness that was usually not fatal. I was deeply affected by his unexpected death. For his obituary, Sister Vigoris asked me to describe his selfless willingness to help his companion Jesuits imprisoned in the concentration camp in Dachau, which I did. As I stood at his grave in the Jesuit cemetery in Pullach in 1951, the memory of our dangerous trips and our close relationship became painfully but tranquilly alive.

Kaspar Quirmbach, SAC

I had already met Father Quirmbach in 1942 when he gave us conferences in the chapel at St. Clara's. His spirituality corresponded to my youthful religious sentiments, but since I felt he

Kaspar Quirmbach, SAC

was almost inapproachable at that time, I was all the more surprised when he said he would be ready to go with me to the plantation at Dachau by bicycle in September, 1944. On that particular day, he was given a load which was just as heavy as mine, and that put us on a kind of common ground.

On the way he told me about his brother Pallottines imprisoned in Dachau. One of them was working in the pepper mill. This made it impossible for him to come to the shop, so we tried to meet him there. The pepper mill stood out in the open and was watched continuously. Extremely nervous and tense, we went past a guard as if we had every right to be there. We ignored the guard at the door in like manner, and he didn't stop us either. I could hardly believe it. Whenever I visited the pepper mill later, I would always carry a package of cigarettes for the guard, himself a prisoner.

During this visit, Father Quirmbach could briefly take care of some business with his companion Pallottine while I stayed in the background. He told me later that the main topic of conversation was the providing for food, since it was only with such help that a prisoner could even hope to survive. We were so exhausted from the dangerous walk to the pepper mill that we rested a little on the way home. That was when the apple incident, already described, took place.

I still remember Father Quirmbach very clearly for more than the trips we took together. I admire him as a priest and a religious, and hold him in high regard for his fatherly kindness and understanding of young people. Before I went to the Novitiate, he humorously told me to try to act just as naturally in the convent as I had when he first got to know me.

God called Father Quirmbach home on July 13, 1966. A member of his community sent me his memorial card, but the memory of this exemplary priest will remain with me long after his death.

The Steinbüchler Family

As I have already mentioned in my account, the Steinbüchler home in Dachau was an oasis from November, 1944 on, a place where I could relax during my journeys and speak freely about what was on my mind.

Mrs. Steinbüchler went to the plantation for the first time in 1943. After that her children, Anneliese (16), Willi (14) and Christl (10) occasionally drove the bicycle to the shop there in order to secretly deliver food which the family had scrimped and saved from their own table. Christl made most of the trips, since the little girl would be less conspicuous, and probably had more time. She went to the prisoners of her own accord and liked to go. A few times I heard her plead, »Mommy, don't you have anything for the prisoners?« I don't know if Mr. Steinbüchler ever went to the market garden. At any rate, he was a convinced opponent of National Socialism, which can be proved by a document from that time which the family saved.

I got to know and appreciate Mrs. Steinbüchler more and more as a wise, sensitive and helpful woman. She came to see us in Freising in the autumn of 1944. Sister Saba, Sister Vigoris and I met with her in Sister Saba's office, and we discussed how we could help the prisoners even more in the days and weeks to come. Mr. Steinbüchler worked in the Wülfert packing house, and Mrs. Steinbüchler suggested that he bring home scraps of lard which she could render for our use in baking.

Mrs. Steinbüchler

Mr. Steinbüchler

Christl Steinbüchler

Anneliese Steinbüchler

Die Deutsche Arbeitsfront

Gau München-Oberbayern

Anschrift des Kreises: Dachau, Ludwig Thomastraße 4a • Drahtanschrift: Arbeitsfront-Dachau
Telefon: Nr. 432

Kreis:
Dachau

Dachau, den 25.9.35.
Ludwig Thomastraße 4a

Herrn

Josef S t e i n b ü c h l e r

D a c h a u

Auf Grund einer Vertrauensratssitzung in dem Betrieb der Firma
Wülfert am 25. ds. kam zur Aussprache, dass Sie in dem Betrieb
dauernd gegen den nationalsozialistischen Staat und dessen Ein
richtung, sowie gegen den Betriebszellenobmann T a u t sich im
mer in einer abfälligen und kritisierenden Weise äussern.
Auf Grund des Gesetzes zur Ordnung der nationalen Arbeit ist e
derart schädigende Handlungsweise für die Betriebsgemeinschaft
zu verwerfen und ich warne Sie zum letzten Mal, Ihr hetzerisch
Treiben aufzugeben.
Sollte der Betriebsfrieden nicht gewahrt bleiben und Sie als S
renfried noch einmal an die Oberfläche tauchen, so sehe ich mi
gezwungen, rücksichtslos gegen Sie einzuschreiten.
Wir dulden nicht, dass das, was unser Führer Adolf Hitler aufb
sowie seine Einrichtung von Menschen, die für den nationalsozi
listischen Staat bisher noch wenig oder garnichts übrig gehabt
ben, verschmäht und bekritelt wird.
Das Ihnen zur gef. Kenntnisnahme.

il H i t l e r!

Kreiswalter.

Then we could save the lard we received through food rationing stamps and use it in baking bread for the prisoners.

After the complete collapse of the »Thousand-Year Reich,« we didn't hear from each other at first, so I was all the more happy when Mrs. Steinbüchler came with Christl to my reception and again to my first profession in Weichs a year later. After I was transferred to Munich in 1948, she visited me regularly for years. She could never get used to my religious name and I was always »Mädi« as far as she was concerned. She pronounced the word with a distinct, loving accent in a way no one else ever could. When her two daughters, who by then were married, eventually gave birth to three grandchildren, she was so busy that our relationship which had developed during that fateful and difficult time broke off temporarily.

In April, 1962, Mrs. Steinbüchler very unexpectedly met me at the entrance of the Third Order Hospital in Munich-Nymphenburg. Christl was in the internal medicine ward at the time and Mrs. Steinbüchler was caring for her sick daughter's children.

◁ *Document from the Nazi Era*

I went at once to visit Christl. In spite of her severe illness, she was full of youth and cheerfulness and still had a characteristic smile in her eyes and at the corners of her mouth. The unexpected visit made both of us happy as we looked at the pictures of Gertrud, her two-year-old daughter. Christl's two children made her very happy and she hoped that she would soon be well enough to go home. But we were never to see each other again. Shortly after that, Mrs. Steinbüchler told me that Christl, only 27 years old, had been called to her eternal home.

After that Mrs. Steinbüchler visited me regularly again. It did both of us good to talk about the past, especially about the time when Christl was able to bring light into many prisoners' dark days as the »Angel of Dachau«. The mother, too, could talk about the painful loss of her youngest daughter.

Later the demands of caring for her grandchildren became so great again that our relationship lessened, but I always remembered this good woman with gratitude and deep respect. She followed her daughter Christl into eternity on April 15, 1975. The words of scripture could also be said of her: »She opened her hand to the needy and reached out her hand to the poor. A woman who fears God deserves praise« (Proverbs 31, 20.30).

Sister Maria Saba Gigl, Local Leader
Sister Maria Vigoris Wolf

From 1942 on, I cared for the orphans and was trained for tailoring at Saint Clara's in Freising as a candidate. Sister Maria Saba Gigl was the local leader and Sister Maria Vigoris Wolf was her assistant. When she was only about 40 years old, Sister Saba, like many religious, lost her teaching position as a result of the National Socialist laws. She cared for the orphans, the elderly Sisters, and the farm. She also looked after us four candidates in a special way, arranging our work and organizing our free time. Through open dialogue, she strove to give us a realistic view of our future life as women religious.

Because she was very interested in all current events, this woman kept us informed about political happenings and war developments, and talked to us about the ideology of National Socialism and its plan to annihilate Christianity and introduce a modern pagan Germanic

religion in its place. Despite her determined opposition to National Socialism, she urged us to restraint and caution in public. When I wanted to wear my black candidate's dress in the Corpus Christi procession in 1944, for example, she did not allow it, thinking it would be exaggerated and unwise for me to display the courage of my convictions on this occasion.

We drew strength and confidence from community prayer. During Compline, the words of Psalm 91, »Whoever dwells in the shelter of the Most High and rests in the shadows of the Almighty says to the Lord, "You are my refuge and my fortress, my God in whom I trust",« were very comforting to me and made my first experience with liturgical prayer a happy one.

Sister Vigoris was a strong and intelligent woman whom we greatly loved and admired. After I had gone to the plantation for the first time and described the appalling conditions in the concentration camp, Sister Saba and Sister Vigoris immediately decided to do everything

◁   Entrance to the Children's Home in Freising:
Second Sister from the left:
Sister M. Saba Gigl, Local Leader
Bottom row, left: Josefa Mack

Sister M. Vigoris Wolf

humanly possible for the prisoners. It was only later that I learned what a difficult responsibility these two Sisters took upon themselves during my »Dachau Year«. The burden of fear and anxiety for me weighed heavily upon them day and night.

Decades later, Mr. and Mrs. Haas and I visited Sister Vigoris in Pullach. Being Karl Leisner's sister and brother-in-law, they wanted to meet her. I had a close relationship with Sister Vigoris until her death in 1980 and I continue to hold her in loving memory.

Sister Saba died in 1958. Like Sister Vigoris, she was a generous woman who was always ready to help. She gave assistance not only to the victims of the concentration camp during the difficult war years, but also to those who had lost everything in the bombing raids, to refugees, and to soldiers returning home.

The two Sisters were able to withstand the difficult times because of the unshakeable trust in God which they shared in common. Today it is almost incomprehensible that these Sisters would take upon themselves the enormous burden of responsibility for regularly sending me off on the dangerous adventure of my Dachau trips. It was an extraordinary time demanding and justifying extraordinary behavior.

It could be seen as a unique coincidence that even though the life journeys of these two Sisters moved in different directions soon after the war, and even though there is more than a twenty-year difference in their death dates, Sister Saba and Sister Vigoris are now resting next to each other in the East Cemetery in Munich. I like to stand at their graves and reflect on the events between 1944 and 1945 and I feel an obligation of perpetual gratitude to both of them.

There are also other names that could be mentioned here, but that would broaden the scope of this account too much. However, the memory of all those persons who stood by me in any way during my trips to the plantation in the concentration camp in Dachau has been indelibly recorded, and I am grateful to each of them.

Looking Back

When people hear about my »Dachau Year«
they often ask, »Were you aware at all of the
danger to which you were letting yourself be
exposed? Weren't you living in constant fear?«
When I think about it, I have to say that fear
was by no means a constant companion. Until
I found my way about the task which I voluntari-
ly undertook, there was so much that was new
and exciting that I really wasn't afraid at first.

There were specific occasions when I did
become greatly frightened, even terrified. For
example, when Father Schönwälder, shaking
with fear, made it clear to me how dangerous it
was to chat with an SS-soldier, or when a guard
suddenly appeared in front of me and demanded to see my papers, or again when Mr. Beer
forbade me to come into his house and com-
municated his own fear to me, or later when I
learned that carrying illegal letters was under
penalty of death and finally when typhoid fever,
something the prisoners feared more than
anything else, was raging in the camp.

The more I heard about the prisoners'
hunger and unspeakable misery, the more my

own fear diminished and my determination to make a total commitment for them increased. I was also spurred on by each expression of gratitude made by these people who had been so badly mistreated, gratitude which was expressed at every opportunity — like the time one of them gave me the beautiful azaleas to take to my parents.

And, strangely enough, during my trips on some spring or summer days, and in the winter, too, when everything was covered with hoarfrost, I experienced the beauty of nature as never before. It was like a compensation for the enormous physical and psychological strain. I remember clearly a dream that was awakened within me by blooming lilacs in a front garden: »How beautiful it must be to be able to marvel at the wonders in God's glorious world when going on a journey that is bright and cheery and free from the threat of war or anxiety for those who are suffering!« This dream let me forget the misery, at least for a little while, and I never lost hope that someday it would come true.

It was also a great help to feel and to know that I was not alone during the dangerous undertaking. I had good companions and when

Sister M. Imma Mack, 1988

I came home after the strenuous and dangerous journeys, I was able to find security in the convent. All the Sisters stood behind my action and supported me whenever possible.

Of course, I gained calmness and strength from a still deeper source. My parents had given me self-confidence and a simple piety. We didn't say long prayers at home and not much was said about God, but everything that we did and were was penetrated with faith and supported by prayer. My faith and trust in God were increased and strengthened in the religious atmosphere at Saint Clara's. Under God's protection I hoped to somehow get through. And I prayed. During the morning Eucharist in the convent chapel at Saint Clara's, I fervently and intensely pleaded for help for the prisoners in Dachau, that the Sisters in the house be protected, and for myself as well.

On the way to the train station, I passed the Vincentians' Munich Chapel in Freising. From the very beginning I had made it a habit of going into this small holy place, recommending

◁ *Marian Shrine in the Munich Chapel in Freising*

my journey to the Mother of God and imploring her for protection and help. From her I received trust and consolation. Once the bicycle was more heavily loaded than usual and I wanted to just drive by and avoid the difficult getting on and off, but I was pulled back as if by an invisible power. After my visit in the chapel, I drove on, greatly consoled. I prayed a lot on the way to the camp, and each time I thanked God from the bottom of my heart that I had gotten through the trip well.

This gratitude has continued throughout my whole life. I cannot express it any better than with the words of the hymn by Joachim Neander:

Praise to our God,
above all things so mightily reigning;
Keeping us safe from all harm,
and so gently sustaining.
Have you not seen All you have needed
has been met by God's gracious ordaining?

(Text: »Lobe den Herren, den mächtigen König,«
Joachim Neander, 1650–1680; Tr. by Catherine Winkwort, 1827–1878, alt.)

Appendix

[1] In his book, THE VICTORY OF FATHER KARL (pp. 151, ff.), Father Otto Pies gives valuable information necessary for understanding my story:

For some time now the priests had maintained a permanent link with the outside world through the civilians who had dealings with people in the workshops and even through some SS men who, forced to join the unit, were inwardly more and more on the side of the prisoners than they were of the Nazi Party. In addition, there was a "little door to life" on the spice plantation and in the agricultural experimental station of the SS. A young priest worked there in the sales store of the greenhouses under the supervision of a gardener employed by the SS. This overseer was quite friendly with the priest, though none the less prudent, and he permitted relatives and friends of the priests to come to the store and leave messages and packages under the pretext of purchasing seeds and plants. This »door to life« was known only to a few reliable persons. But back and forth through this door came a steady stream of news, food supplies, medicine and other things. The traffic was cleverly organized ... a secret self-help program through which immeasurable blessings were transmitted without the knowledge of the SS or other overseers. Through this message center, contact was also established with the Archbishop of Munich and the objects necessary for the ceremony of ordination (of Karl Leisner) brought into the camp.

A young girl, a candidate in a convent in Freising, became the most important link between the camp and the outside world. With a childlike trust in God's protection and completely carefree, she would make the difficult and dangerous trips to the camp that made it possible for the necessary preparations to be made and the required authorizations to be transmitted. It was she of whom Cardinal Faulhaber spoke in 1945 when in a speech on heroism he extolled a young woman whose courage had contributed to mitigating the suffering in Dachau and to the successful ordination of a priest in the concentration camp ...

This candidate took it upon herself to establish the difficult connections between the priests' block and the Most Reverend Cardinal, as well as any contact with the homeland at all ...

[2] KL was the official abbreviation for concentration camp at the time.

[3] The »pepper mill« was a large wooden shed in which the herbs and spices harvested from the plantation were processed and packed for purchase.

[4] In the article, »Memories of the Last Months of World War II« (»Erinnerungen an die letzten Monate des zweiten Weltkriegs«), written for the »Dachau Circular« (»Dachauer Rundbriefe«) in 1968, Father Zawacki, SJ, described this visit with Cardinal Faulhaber as follows:

An ordination was to take place in the camp, since a French bishop was also imprisoned there. The permission of the Archbishop of Munich-Freising, the holy oils and some other articles were needed for the ordination. The active intermediary for this task was a very young woman, Josefa Mack, who was a postulant with the Poor School Sisters of Notre Dame stationed at Saint Clara's Convent in Freising. I knew of her activities, but each one usually worked alone for reasons of security. This time, however,

154

I was to go with her to the Archbishop, present the prisoners' request, introduce the young woman and recommend her as being trustworthy. Cardinal Faulhaber received us with great kindness and understanding. After I had briefly given him the information, he said that he was in agreement and that I didn't have to do anymore about it. I heard only later that everything went as planned.

[5] Account by Father Ferdinand Schönwälder in THE VICTORY OF FATHER KARL, pp. 152, ff. (slightly edited and somewhat abridged):

It was on a foggy, gray November morning (Nov. 23, 1944) that Father Pies informed me that he would like to do everything possible to see that his friend Leisner be ordained as a priest before the year was out. It was difficult for me to grasp the meaning of his words. But Father Pies often had sudden inspirations ... We were together in a work detail on the roll call area waiting for the guards who were to escort us to our work site. Father Pies let me in on his plans: I was to help establish contact with the outside world. At that time I had an inside job which gave me an opportunity to meet civilians, and thanks to Providence I also had a close and permanent contact with the Convent of the Poor School Sisters in Freising ... each week a candidate from this cloister, the present Sister Imma, known to us under her alias, »Mädi«, would come to the camp to bring altar wine and communion wafers for the Polish priests who at that time had to celebrate Mass secretly and bring Holy Communion to the other prisoners ... Mädi had to take two important letters necessary for the ordination of Karl Leisner, one to his Eminence, Cardinal Faulhaber ... and the other for the Jesuit Brother Zawacki. The latter was asked to accompany Mädi when

155

she went to Cardinal Faulhaber and to confirm her credibility there. The cardinal gave the requested permission with a surprising swiftness. At that time Bishop Gabriel Piguet of Clermont-Ferrand in France, who was to officiate at the consecration, was a prisoner in the camp. The ordination ceremony was scheduled for the Third Sunday in Advent in 1944. The candidate for the priesthood at that time lay seriously ill in the camp hospital.

Father Pies took care of him with a dedicated love ... The Superior in Freising, Sister Saba, and her Sisters took care of procuring the most necessary medicine and food ... Mädi came twice weekly, overburdened with medicines and food supplies. It occurred to me sometimes that the Sisters were depriving themselves of many things ... A week before the ordination, Leisner could move about in the infirmary a little. All that was lacking now were the necessary consecrated oils and the liturgical books. Mädi also brought these and we smuggled them into the camp secretly.

Deacon Karl Leisner was — as planned — ordained a priest on the Third Sunday of Advent. At his First Mass his first blessings were for the Sisters in Freising, and especially for our brave little Mädi ...

6 According to the legend, St. Tarcisius (meaning »I am courageous«) lived in Rome during the third century. The twelve-year-old was an altar boy and after the celebration of Eucharist, he brought consecrated hosts hidden in a container under his clothing to Christians waiting in prison for their imminent execution. He was attacked by a pagan mob one day and beaten to death.